20 Great Persons of the World

20 Great Persons of the World

Sumer Chand

Manas Publications
(We Convert Fighters into Writers)
New Delhi - 110 002 (INDIA)

MANAS PUBLICATIONS
(We Convert Fighters into Writers)
(Publishers, Library Suppliers, Importers & Exporters)
4402/5-A, Ansari Road (Opp. HDFC Bank)
Darya Ganj, New Delhi - 110 002 (India)
Phones: Off.: 011-23260783, 23265523, Res.: 011-23842660
E-mail: manaspublications@gmail.com
manaspublications@yahoo.com
Website: www.manaspublications.in

ISBN 978-81-7049-488-1
₹ 595.00

Designed at
Manas Publications

Printed in India at
R.K. Printers, Delhi
and published by Mrs Suman Lata for
Manas Publications, 4402/5-A,
Ansari Road (Opp HDFC Bank),
Darya Ganj, New Delhi - 110002 (INDIA)

Preface

The universe came into being 1,97,29,49,110 years ago. Since then, there have been many religious, social, political and warrior great persons in the world. The people do not know about them. If at all they know, they know only about those who concern them. The religious people know about the persons of their religion and not the great men of other religions. People know about few great men who did remarkable work for their society and certainly not about them who did commendable work for other societies. Similarly people know about the great persons of their country and know little about the great persons of other countries. I was contemplating for the last several years to write about all the great people of the world – religious, warriors, social and political personalities or otherwise. But I do not know how I bypassed this task for other two-three books. Truly, the task was so stupendous and difficult to undertake that I hesitated to take it in my hands. But, this summer when I went to my mountain abode at Tangdhar, I took cajole to start this work.

Firstly, I prepared a list of great men from all walks of life throughout the world. It took three days to contemplate on the list. I selected twenty personalities, well-known in the world in their own sphere.

At first I concentrated on the major religions prevalent in the world. Founder of a religion must be a great person because billions of people are following him. Of course, it is not an ordinary achievement that so many people found him worth following. Major religions of the world are Christian, Islam, Hindu, Bauddha, Jain and Sikh. It is quite surprising that Hindu religion has no founder and it is still a religion. Therefore I took the founders of Christian, Islam, Bauddha, Jain and Sikh religions. Zoroastrians known as Parsi are few millions in number. There is a hotchpotch and Ibrahim is said to be the founder of Judaism. But Christianity and Islam also go to the doors of Ibrahim. Therefore, I could not dare to include him in my list.

In India, two personalities – Swami Vivekananda and Swami Dayananda – also gave the lead to their ideas on crores of followers. They have been narrated in the book. Next came the persons who were the citadel of courage and turned the tides in their favour by their mental and physical fortitude. I included Fidel Castro, Subhas Chandra Bose, Alexander the Great and Adolf Hitler. I also included those who did wonders for suppressed humanity. They are Abraham Lincoln, Nelson Mandela, Martin Luther King Junior, Vladimir Lenin and Mao Tse-tung. Renowned philosophers, who guided humanity with their ideas and ideals are also included. They are Rousseau, Plato and Aristotle. I tried to do justice to each of them so that readers know all about them at one place. So the readers are the best judge of my work.

B-1, Industrial Estate Sumer Chand
Sonepat (Haryana)

Contents

Jesus Christ

JESUS CHRIST was the founder of the Christian religion. He is said to have been born to a virgin – Mary. Mary was engaged to marry Joseph, son of David.

The angel Gabriel, sent by God, said to Mary: "God has blessed you and is pleased with you. Don't be afraid, you will become impregnated by the Holy Spirit and give birth to a baby boy and you will call him Jesus."

King Caesar Augustus wanted to have a list of all the people in the empire, to make sure they paid their taxes. He ordered everyone to return to the town where their families originally came from, and enter their names in a register there. Mary and Joseph travelled a long way from Nazareth to Bethlehem. They travelled very slowly because Mary's baby was due to be born soon.

Joseph was worried when he found out that Mary was expecting a baby before their marriage had taken place. He wondered if he should put off the wedding altogether. Then an angel appeared in his dream and explained that Mary had been chosen by God to be the mother of his son and told Joseph that the baby would be named Jesus. When

Joseph woke up, he did what the angel had told him to do and took Mary as his wife.

When they reached Bethlehem they had problems finding a place to stay. So many people had come to register their names, that every house and inns were full. The only shelter they got was a stable with animals. In this poor place Mary gave birth to Jesus, the Son of God. Jesus' bed was the manger that the animals ate their hay from.

In the hills and fields outside Bethlehem, shepherds looked after their sheep through the long night. As the new day began, suddenly an angel appeared before them. The shepherds were very scared, but the angel said, "Don't be afraid. I have good news for you and everyone. Today in Bethlehem a Saviour has been born for you. You will find the baby lying in a manger."

Then the shepherds decided to go to Bethlehem to see what has happened. So the shepherds went to Bethlehem and found Mary and Joseph. The baby Jesus was lying in a manger as they had been told. When they saw him, they told everyone what the angel had said and everyone who heard the story was astonished. Then the shepherds returned to their sheep, praising God for sending his Son to be their Saviour.

Herod, the king of Judea, heard this and it made him very angry to think that someone might take his place as king. Herod sent his men to search the child. His men found the house where Jesus with Mary were staying, they bowed down and worshipped him. They were warned in a dream, by God, not to go back to Herod. So they returned home to their countries. After their departure, an angel appeared in Joseph's dream and advised him to escape to Egypt with Jesus and Mary. During the night they left for Egypt, where they stayed until Herod died.

When Herod realized that he had been tricked by his men, he was furious and he gave orders to kill all the boys aged two or younger in Bethlehem and the surrounding area. This was to try and kill the Jesus.

After Herod had died, Joseph had another dream in which an angel appeared to him and said, "Get up, take Jesus and Mary and go back to Israel, for those who were trying kill Jesus are dead."

So Joseph got up, took Jesus and Mary and they went back to Israel. But when he heard that Herod's son was now king of Judea, he was afraid to go there. So instead they went to Galilee, and lived in their old town of Nazareth.

A man named John the Baptist came there and baptized Jesus. And as soon as Jesus was baptized the sky opened up and a voice from heaven said, "This is my Son, I love him and I am pleased with him."

He was given the power by the God to do the work for which he was sent. He was given authority over all the works of Satan, Sin, Disease, Demons and even Death. He had all the powers – physical, spiritual, mental and emotional. He went down to Capernaum, a town in Galilee and on the Sabbath, began to teach people. They were amazed at his teachings, because his message had all the authority. There was a man possessed by evil spirit. He cried, "Have you come to destroy us." At this Jesus said, "Do not cry, come out of him." Then the demon came out without injuring the man. All the people were amazed and said – "He can even give orders to the evil spirits and they obey him." This news spread in the surrounding areas.

At the same time Jesus began to preach. While he was walking by the sea of Galilee he saw two brothers who were fishermen – Peter and Andrew. He took them with him. Similarly two brothers were on a ship mending their nets – James and John. They were also taken with him. He went from one synagogue to another to preach the gospel and cure the sick people. His fame spread throughout Syria. The people brought to him all kinds of sick and those possessed by evil spirits. Lunatics suffering from palsy were brought to him and they were cured. A great multitude followed him and he went to the mountain, sat there and preached and blessed the poor people. Those who were mourning their dead were comforted. Those who were hungry and thirsty were blessed. Those who needed mercy were granted. The people with pure hearts were blessed to see God. He said that a candle put under a bushel cannot give light but it should be on the stand for giving light.

Another story is told about a man with leprosy. While Jesus was in a town, a man came to him and said – "if you are willing, you can make me clean." And immediately leprosy left the man. This news also spread and the people began to come to hear him and to be healed of their sickness. But Jesus often withdrew to lonely places and prayed.

Another story is told of a paralytic person. One day when he was preaching, Pharisees and teachers of law, who had come from every village of Galilee, Judea and Jerusalem, some men came carrying a paralytic man. He was laid before Jesus. When Jesus saw their faith, he said, "friend, your sins are forgiven." The Pharisees and teachers of law saw this and began thinking to themselves, "who is this fellow who speaks blasphemy? Who can forgive the sins but the God only." Jesus knew their feelings and asked them, "why are you thinking these things in your hearts?" The son of the God has known to do this; He said to the man, "You get up and go." He immediately stood up and walked away. At this also, the people were amazed and praised him along with the God. They were filled with awe and said, "we have seen quite surprising things today." There is another story of converting water in to wine. There was a wedding, he and his mother were invited there. Incidentally, the wine ran short. His mother asked him to do the needful. There was a very big jar. He asked the servants to fill it with water. They did. He asked them to draw some and take to the guests. When the master guest tasted, it was very good wine. He thus, revealed his glory and the people put their faith in him.

Once Jesus went to the far shore of the sea. The crowd followed him because they saw miracles he performed on the sick. Then he went to the hillside and sat down with his disciples. The Jewish Passover feast was near. Jesus saw a large crowd coming to him. He said to his disciple, "where, shall we buy bread for these all to eat?" His disciple answered, "Even eight months' wages would not buy enough bread for each one to have a bite." Jesus asked them to sit for eating. They were about five thousand of them. They sat on the grass. Jesus took five loaves of bread and distributed it to the sitting crowd. When they all had enough, he asked his disciples to gather the remaining loaves so that the remaining may not go waste. The crowd proclaimed, "He is surely a Prophet." He preached the gospel of the God and said, those who follow it shall be more righteous than the scribes and Pharisees and shall enter the kingdom of the heaven. They, who are angry with their brothers, without cause shall be in danger of hell fire. He advised the people not to commit adultery, otherwise they will go to hell. He said, even if your right hand offends the women, cut it. If your right eye offends the women then pluck it out. He said, you have heard, eye for an eye and a tooth, for a tooth but I say, you resist not evils, but who shall ever smite you on the right cheek offer him the left also. If a man sues you by law and takes away your coat, offer him your cloak also. If someone compels you to go a mile, go two miles with him. You say, love your neighbour and hate your enemy but I say, love your enemy too.

By this way, he performed so many miracles. Those who followed Jesus held different positions in society and came from different cultures. It was not love and compassion, which Jesus showed through his miracles, which drew them, they chose to follow Jesus, because they believed him to be son of God who came to set them free from sins in their lives.

He once said,

"Whatever you donate, it should not be publicised, but should be secret. If you do, it is hypocrisy. It is not a glory to talk it in streets. When you do it, your left hand should not know what the right hand has done. The God knows it and will reward it properly openly. The prayer to the God should also be secret, because the God rewards such prayers. The prayers should also not be repeated, because he knows everything without speaking loudly. The God knows your needs and he is capable of doing everything for you. The only prayer should be – give us bread for today and forgive us our debits as we forget out debtors. Please do not lead us to temptations and save us from evils. When you fast do not make it a show that you are at fast because He knows it and would reward it. Do not keep your treasure here on earth – a moth can eat it, thieves can steal it, keep it in heaven safe with the God, where there is your treasure your own heart will be there itself – it will be with the God. Do not keep your eye on evil because it causes darkness."

Jesus and his eleven disciples ate the Passover meal together. He told his disciples, "Look, the hour is near and the son of man is betrayed into hands of sinners." While he was still speaking, Judas, one of the twelve disciples arrived. With him was a large crowd with swords, clubs, sent by the chief priests and the elders of the people. Now the betrayer had arranged a signal with them, "The one I kiss, is the man, arrest him." Jesus replied, "Friends, do what you have come for." He was arrested. The men who were guarding Jesus, began mocking and beating him. They blindfolded him and demanded 'Prophesy' who hit you? They also said many insulting things to him.

At day break, the elders of the people, the chief priests and teachers of the law met together. Having been tried and sentenced to death, Jesus was beaten with thirty nine strips on his back and then was forced to walk to the place of execution. They came to a place called the skull. There he was crucified. At this Jesus said, "Father, forgive them, for they do not know what they are doing." His body was placed in a tomb, cut out of a rock.

There was a violent earthquake. An angel of God came down from heaven and went into the tomb. The guards were afraid. His disciples were talking of him and they say he was out of the tomb and came to them. They were quite surprised and took him as a ghost. But after some time Jesus was successful to make them understand the reality. He was alive after three days.

They say next time Jesus remained on earth for forty days. During this period he gave authority to his disciples to carry on his work. Jesus was born in the area where Jews were living and were carrying on the faith in their religion. Therefore it was quite a tough to initiate a new religion there. This was the reason why he was sentenced to death. After resurrection, he asked his disciples to carry his work forward for the sake of humanity. He built the first church where his tenets were taught to the people.

After his death, Christianity came to reality. This new religion spread to far off places. Presently, entire Europe follows Christianity and its followers are spread throughout the world. The churches are in every country and the priests preach the teaching of Jesus Christ. The Christ means, the son of the God.

Once Jesus met a very rich person who requested Jesus to tell him the way to go to heaven. At that Jesus told him to distribute his wealth to the poor and then come to him. At this, the wealthy person hesitated to do what he was told to do. Then Christ said, "It is possible that a camel passes through a ring but it is not possible that a rich man goes to the heaven."

Jesus gave his power of healing to his disciples. They were: Simon, who was called Peter, and Andrew his brother; James and his brother John; Philip and Bartholomew; Thomas and Matthew, the tax collector; James and Thaddaeus. He told them to cure the sick, cleanse the lepers, raise the dead, cast out the devils.

His teachings were: Do not keep gold and silver with you, not even brass. Shake off the dust from your shoes when you leave a house you lived in and a city you stayed at. He said I am leaving you like a sheep among the wolves. Therefore be wise enough like a serpent and harmless like a dove. He said that time is coming when the brother will kill a brother, a father his child and children will kill their parents. He cautioned his disciples that they would be hated because of him. Whatever I tell you in darkness, say it in light, whatever I tell you in your ears, say it from the posts of the houses. You are valuable, therefore escape being caught by those who are after me. He commanded his disciples and they left for preaching.

Jesus was a great person and that is why millions of people are his followers throughout the world even after more than two thousand years. The Christ Era was started after his name which is the International measurement of the time period.

Prophet Mohammad

PROPHET MOHAMMAD was born in the Quresh dynasty of Arabia. The Quresh were very respectable and well to do people of the area. Almost sixty dynasties earlier, Ismail was born in the same dynasty. Prophet Mohammad was born in c 570 in Macca town. It was the same baby for which Hazrat Ibrahim and Hazrat Ismail prayed to Allah. It was same baby about which Gautam Buddha whispered in the ears of his disciple Nanda at his last time. Nanda asked Gautam Buddha after you are gone who will guide the world. At this Gautam Buddha whispered "Nanda I am not first Buddha nor I am the last Buddha. After me another Buddha would come for this purpose."

His father was Hazrat Abdullah and mother was Bibi Aminah. His grandfather Hazrat Abdul Muttalib named him Mohammad which means the person who is admired the most. He also hoped that this boy would one day or the other, prove to be most famous. He proved he was right. The whole world knows Mohammad. His father died when he was not even born and when he was six years old his mother also died. His grandfather undertook his rearing but unfortunately after two years he also died. His uncle Hazrat Abu Talib took responsibility to look after him. He cared for him more than his own sons. During those days there was no system of education.

Therefore, Mohammad was illiterate. Since his uncle was a trader, he learnt trading and gradually rose to be a young man.

Hazrat Khadija was a rich lady. She was a widow at that time. She was in trade. Mohammad was made incharge of her trade by her due to the fair and honest dealings by him. He was honest and hard working. She was so impressed by him that she married him despite the fact that she was 40 years old and Mohammad was 25. This was an unique happening.

That period was of blind following and of idol worship. The character of the people was at the lowest ebb. The people were slaves of every type of evil. Mohammad constantly thought, how can that be reformed. For this he needed aloofness. At about three miles from Macca there was a cave named Hira. Mohammad used to hide himself there to remember Allah. It was the month of Ramadan. Hazrat Jibrail appeared before him. He was the messenger of Allah. He said, read. Mohammad said – I am not literate. At this Jibrail shook him greatly and when he was tired a lot, he again said – read. Mohammad again replied – I am not literate. Jibrail again shook him as before and said – read. Jibrail repeated the shaking thrice and said – read in the name of Allah and your protector is supreme who taught everything to man which he did not know.

This was the first message of Allah and he was 41 years old at that time. Hazrat Jibrail did not come for six months and Mohammad continued to go to Hira cave.

The second message came after six months. The message was: Arise and tell the people about the supremacy of Allah and do not believe in idols. Do not be kind to those who are after gaining more and more.

Mohammad carried the message to the people that Allah is only one who is worth woi shipping. One should live a selfless and greedless life.

During those days it was very a difficult job to carry this message. There were 360 idols at Kaaba, one each was worshipped every day.

The people were adamant to follow the old traditions. They were not even ready to listen to him. Still due to his good past behaviour, some embraced him with love and faith and all did not hesitate to devote everything for him. He was the first Musalman. Musalman means, the one who has the faith in Allah only. His wife Hazrat Khadija, Hazrat Ali, his cousin, Hazrat Zayd his personal server and his friend Hazrat Abu Bakr were some who accepted his message. Thus, his message spread gradually and the number of Musalmans increased day-by-day. This, he was not doing so openly but by personal contact only. There is an episode of his boyhood. This is the principle of God that he keeps the one pure and spotless to whom he is to assign some great task, so that others cannot raise a finger at him. Because Mohammad was to become prophet in the coming days and for a prophet it is necessary that his life should be quite pure and sin free, therefore Allah made his life virtuous and of sound character. Once, the walls of Kaaba were being repaired. The boys were taking part along with the adults in this work. Mohammad and his uncle were among the volunteers. Hazrat Abbas suggested him to take off his Tehmad (a cloth used in place of pantaloon) and place it on the shoulders so that the stones may not injure the shoulder. It was not a new thing in the Arab weather. He took off his Tehmad and put it on the shoulder. But he at once thought of his nakedness. He fell unconscious on the ground. When he came to the senses, he cried "my Tehmad, my Tehmad, my Tehmad". The people there, wrapped his Tehmad round his waist. Then after some time he became normal. Thus Allah kept him away from shortcomings and sins so that he did not hinder his good work in future. Allah inspired Mohammad to take part only in good works. He took part in the peace talks of Fazal. It was decided there.

We shall irradicate the violence from the country.

We should protect the pilgrims.

We shall help the poor and destitute.

We shall side with those who are exploited.

We shall not allow in Macca those, who are against justice and peace.

These proposals were taken up at his suggestions. Due to his bent of mind toward righteousness, he adopted the business of gentlemen and always carried it out quite fairly. It was here that that the people took him to be a worthy person. In that profession he did not do any sort of bungling as the others usually do in the trade. His fair dealings stood him in good stead in spreading the message of the God – Allah, in future. It was quite natural that the public in general, took him for a good person to be relied at once.

But due to the character of the public in general being at the lower level, Mohammad had to face great difficulty in spreading the message of Allah in Macca and around. But he did not hesitate and carried on steadfastly.

After three years, one day Mohammad climbed Saffa mountain and started speaking loudly. This is particularly done at the time of an imminent danger. The people collected there and he said – "If I say that a big army is behind the mountain to attack you, will you believe me?"

The people said, "Yes, because you have not told any lie."

He continued, "My fellow men I want to attract you towards Allah and detract you from idol worship. If you do not agree with me then I warn you of great danger and punishment."

This was the first announcement about Islam. At this the people – Quresh, as they were known, started whispering and talking among themselves. Only forty or so people had adopted Islam upto that time. One day he went inside Kaaba and announced about the only one God, Allah. Riots started there. The people attacked him. Hazrat Ibne Abi Halla came to his help. Many swords were charged at him and he was killed then and there. This was the first sacrifice for Islam.

His message did not suit the Quresh because it was a challenge to their hegemony. Therefore, they opposed Mohammad tooth and nail. It is true that once a new order comes, the old order opposes it. No one wants to give up its place. This has always happened. Therefore it was quite natural, this was to happen.

He was opposed by following manners.

1. They laughed at the message and the holy book Quran.
2. They declared Mohammad a fanatic and his message, the words from a fool.
3. When his arguments were not properly answered, they resorted to force?
4. When they did not succeed, they resorted to harm him physically? Thorns were spread on his way. Filth was thrown at him. Rubbish was placed at him. Once, he was even throttled. But this did not deter him and rather helped him.
5. When they did not succeed, they tried to sabotage his programme from within by showing sympathy?
6. Again they did not succeed. Therefore they started using force against him and his followers.
7. When the message reached out of Macca, they united in a big way and warned the people against the new Prophet.
8. When it was all futile they came down to purchasing the truth by mutual treaty. But they failed.

When the opponents saw that the power of Islam had started to increase, they resorted to the policy of suppression with very strong hands. They put those who adopted Islam, on hot sand for hours together and placed very heavy stones on their breast. They used different methods of brutalities, which were prevalent during those days. Look at the samples of those brutalities:

One day the Quresh put Hazrat Khabbab on the burning coal and at this one strong person put his foot on the breast so that he could not move either side. They carried on this till the coal became cold under him.

Hazrat Bilal was also put on the hot sand at noon time and a very heavy stone was placed on his chest. He was asked to give up Islam or otherwise he would die in that state by inches. But he murmured that

Allah is the only one to be worshipped. A very long rope was tied to his neck and dozen of youth used to drag him throughout the town, from one end to the other. But he did not bow. The Qureshes put Hazrat Umar on hot sand and he was beaten till he fell unconscious. But he did not retract.

When Hazrat Usman became Musalman his uncle tied him by a rope and thrashed him to the extent of last limit.

Hazrat Umar, before he himself turned Musalman, used to tie with strong rope, Hazrat Sad Ibn Zaid and his wife, who was the sister of Hazanat Umar and asked them to renounce Islam. But they both stood fast and did not move a bit.

This brutual suppression created such a situation that those who were making the mind to turn to Islam, hesitated and they were put on hold. Decidedly this was a great hindrance in spreading Islam among the Quresh.

When Mohammad saw that the things were going beyond levels of tolerance and he was unable to carry out the message of Allah properly, he decided to send some of his followers to Ethopia. The benefit of this move was that the people who had turned to Islam would be safe there at least till the time they came back. The other point was that these followers would spread the message of Islam to the places they go. Thus, many persons took the journey to Ethopia. The king of Ethopia who was known as Nijashi gave peaceful protection to these pilgrims.

When Quresh knew about this protection of Muslims by Ethopia, they sent their message to Nijashi. Nijashi called the Muslims to him and asked what new religion had they adopted?

Muslims nominated Hazrat Jaffar as their representative to talk to king Nijashi. Jaffar told the king:

"Oh! the king, we were wandering under ignorance and sinfully. We were worshipping hundred of idols instead of one Allah. We used to eat the dead bodies, commit thefts and were violent towards others. The strong one felt proud in suppressing the weaker one. Our life was worse than even the animals. It is the grace of Allah that he changed our life. Allah gave birth to such a person who is out of us and we know him since his birth Allah made him his own messenger. He is truly honest and quite fair even to his enemies. We accepted his saintliness and righteousness. He asked us to be Muslim instead of worshiping idols he advised us to worship only the Allah. He asked us to tell the truth and leave thefts and sinful acts, to help the needy and destitutes to spend our savings in the service of Allah. We obeyed him and left idol worship and we worship only Allah and abstain from bad deals and actions. At this our own people turned enemy for us. They were forcing us to convert back to our old faith. We left our places and came to your kingdom. Therefore the Quresh sent the message to you for our recall."

At this the king asked to recite some part of the message of Allah sent through their prophet. Hazrat Jaffar recited some quotes. This brought tears in the eyes of the king and he said, "By Allah these preachings are preachings of Angels are the two flames of the same truth." He refused to send back the Muslims.

Next day the Quresh again went to the king and requested him to ask the opinion of these people about Hazrat Isa because they were aware that Muslims do not accept Isa as the son of God and instead they said he was the son of Mariyam. It was pure and simple diplomacy. This could turn the king against the Muslims.

The king again called the Muslims to him and asked about Hazrat Isa. Hazrat Jaffar told the king very frankly that their Prophet Mohammad told them that Hazrat Isa was the servant of God and was his messenger. When the king heard this he picked up a straw and said: "But God Isa was like this straw in comparison to your Prophet." Thus, this diplomacy of the Quresh failed and Muslims lived there peacefully. Their numbers also increased to 83.

This was one aspect. On the other hand those who deserted the enemies also adopted the message of Islam. This was not due to any greed and duress but due to the factual position of his preachings.

The situation became so favourable that even Hazrat Hamza and Hazrat Umar turned Muslims. This was a great blow to Quresh and it was a great sensation. The opponents of Islam were greatly disappointed. At this Muslims were encouraged. So far, they were not so openly performing Namaz etc, but now they were boldly doing it. While it was not at all possible to perform Namaz at Kaaba but now many persons together started performing the Namaz there without fear.

The head of the Quresh was greatly startled and had long consultations with the advisers to crush Islam. It was declared that one who has dealings with the new Prophet would be an out caste. Even eatables were also banned for him. The one who would handover him to the head of Quresh for killing would be rewarded and these bans on his followers would be effective till the time he was killed. This order was pasted on the gate of Kaaba. How dangerous was this move to nib Islam.

At this Mohammad moved to a valley with his family. This valley was known as Shabe Abi Talib. Thus, the move of the opponents failed. The other Musalmans also moved there. They spent very miserable days for three years there. A time came when they had to survive on tree leaves. When the children cried due to hunger, Quresh felt very happy – seeing the pitiable situation of these persons. But their social boycott ended when some merciful out of them thought very coolly over the unhuman treatment meted to them.

Two tragedies decended on Mohammad one after the other. His uncle Abu Talib died suddenly and after few months his wife Hazrat Khadija died. Both of them were like shields to him. Therefore these deaths caused him great harm. With them he always felt safe but now he felt a bit lonely. Two things were side by side. The cruelty, barbarity and rudeness of Quresh intensified his devotion for spreading the message of Allah progressed day and night. He thought that the message should also go out of Macca. Therefore he travelled to Tayaf, forty mile away from Macca. This was a very prosperous town with rich people but unfortunately he was not taken seriously there too. Head of a clan even said, "Did the Allah not find any messanger better than you. We cannot even talk to you. If at all you are true then it is beyond our culture to talk to you and if you are telling a lie then you are not fit even to see your face." The true message of Allah was laughed at. They not only did not listen to him but they instigated the lampoons to throw stones at him. He was very badly injured and oozing blood filled his shoes. Those criminals continued beating and calling him choicest names. Somehow he took shelter in a garden. But it was his courage and steadfast resolve which stood him in good stead and he continued.

He was determined to spread the message of Allah with courage and devotion to as many people as possible. He used to meet all the clans at the time of Hajj and convey to them the teachings of Islam – the only way to make the life successful. In the same manner wherever there were large annual fairs in Arabia, he used to go there and preach Islam. By this manner he could win the hearts of the people and the people reposed their confidence in him.

As the message of Islam reached to a large area, it also reached Medina. There were two clans – Aws and Khazraj. Yahudis were living around them. After ten years of preaching in Macca, the Muslims, at the command of their Prophet, migrated to Medina. Mohammad started telling the people there that there is a mention of the coming of a second messenger in your religious books. Why don't you believe your own religious book? They took Mohammad to be the same messenger as mentioned in their book and relied on what ever he told them. This helped him greatly.

The main points of Islam taught to people were:

1. Only Allah is worth worshipping and no one else.
2. We shall not steal.

3. We shall not rape.
4. We shall not kill our babies.
5. We shall not falsely accuse anyone.
6. We shall truly follow what the messenger of Allah tells us.

He said if you follow these principles then you are sure to achieve heaven other wise it is up to Allah how he treats you.

When Islam became a power and the number of Musalmans increased, it was felt that a directory be prepared which can be useful for Islamic way of life. The directions at that time were:

1. Allah only is supreme no one else be compared to him.
2. Respect the parents and obey them.
3. The relatives, poor and travellers be given their full rights and no injustice be done to them.
4. One should neither be extravagant nor be a miser.
5. The babies should not be killed for fear of poverty, Allah would feed them.
6. There should be no rape so that the society may be pure and crime free.
7. No one's life may be taken without a cogent reason so that peace prevails in society.
8. Proper treatment be done to orphans.
9. Promises are to be truly fulfilled because there is an account of promises with Allah.
10. All measurements and weighing scales be always true.
11. One should not listen to rumours as this spoils the relations.
12. One should not be proud because it is very bad behaviour.

There was a conspiracy to kill Mohammad. Quresh of Macca planned to attack him when he came out of this house in morning. But he planned to go to Medina and he confided this to Hazrat Ali. He also asked him to use his bed so that Quresh were under the impression that he is there. He sneaked out of the house at night and took Hazrat Abu Bakr with him. They went in the Guffa (cave) of Saur and remained there for three days. On the fourth day they came out, and travelled day and night for Medina.

After coming to Medina he laid the foundation of a mosque and raised its walls with the help of others. This mosque is known as Masjid Nabui. He spread brotherhood there among the locals and those who shifted from Macca due to sufferings there.

But Quresh did not let it lie down. They wanted to punish him and crush his movement. He was opposed with greater force.

There was a great tussle between the two. Even battles were fought. Yahudis also stood in his opposition for fear of loss of their influence and trade in their areas. He had to fight on two fronts. But Yahudis compromised on certain terms. He sent letter to the king of Rome and also to the king of Iran in favour of his mission – spreading the message of Allah. Ultimately his followers had victory over Macca from where he was forced to go to Medina. Then the idea of Hajj came to his mind. As soon as the people knew it, a big crowd of followers came to go with him. He took a bath and started on the she camel. He announced in the loud voice: Oh Allah we are ready for you, oh Allah we are ready for you – You have no other to share with you – we are present before you – all praise for you. Thousands of people spoke to him. It was a great sentimental scene. He thus proceeded gradually and reached Macca and when he saw Kaaba he uttered:

"Oh, Allah, bestow upon us your great honour and greatness."

He took a round of Kaaba and offered Namaz. After morning Namaz he delivered his historic lecture which is the vital part of his teachings.

Summary of his speech is:

The Principle of ignorance is under my feet.

Arab and non-Arab have no superiority over each other. You all are the progeny of Adam who was born out of the earth.

Every Musalman is the brother of the other Musalman.

Feed your servants with whatever you eat – whatever you wear, give them the same to wear.

Every killing before the arrival of Islam is condoned. Do not take any revenge.

Every interest before arrival of Islam is remitted.

You have rights on women and women have rights on you. Therefore be afraid of Allah with regard to women.

Your blood and your property is a curse to others until doomsday.

I am leaving one important thing of Allah for you – that is the Quran, the book of Allah.

After this he looked to the crowd and asked:

"When you go to Allah and He asks you about me, what will you tell?"

The crowd cried:

"You have taken the message of Allah to us fully well and did your duty well."

He raised his finger to the sky and said – "Allah be witness."

He cited the quotation of Quran at this occasion:

"Today, I have completed the work of religion and have done my duty and you have accepted Islam as a religion."

On the occasion of this Hajj, he himself told all the methods of Hajj and did everything himself.

On this occasion he also told: "Learn the methods of Hajj from me. I do not know whether I shall come for another Hajj or not."

On this occasion he told to the Musalmans:

"Those who are here tell this to those who are not here: Mohammad was sent for a purpose to let the truth prevail over the untruth. That purpose was over."

There was a recall from Allah. His health deteriorated. It was Wednesday and up to Monday his disease became serious.

When his health improved a bit he spoke the last sentence of life: The Allah has given right to the man – either he should posses the worldly things or accept whatever is available with Allah.

He thanked Abu Bakr: "He is the true friend of mine out of my followers."

He uttered many times: "With the people who are blessed by Allah."

He passed away at the age of 63. Crores of Muslims are his followers.

Hazrat Khadija was his first wife. After her death he married the daughter of Hazrat Abu Bakr, Hazrat Aaisa and daughter of Hazrat Jumma, Hazrat Sooda. His other wives were – Hazrat Zaniat, Hazrat Salima, Hazrat Zaniat Baneet, Hazrat Judeer, Hazrat Mamuna and Hazrat Safiya. His another wife was Jukaneer who was from Egypt.

All his children were from his first wife Hazrat Khadija. A son was also born to Hazrat Maria who died in childhood. All the three sons from Hazrat Khadija died at the young age. There were other four daughters, youngest daughter was Hazrat Fatima who had two sons Hazrat Hassan and Hazrat Hussain. These two became very famous in the Muslim world.

Gautam Buddha

GAUTAM BUDDHA was the founder of the Bauddha religion. He was born in 563 BC at Lumbini near Kapilavastu in Nepal. His father was Suddhodana and mother was Mahamaya who died 7 days after his birth. His earlier name was Siddharth. He was looked after by second wife of Suddhodana, Mahaprajapati. At the time of his naming ceremony eight scholars who suggested the name Siddharth, had in their minds that the child would be a great man after achieving renunciation. Another Sadhu also had a prophecy that either Siddharth will be a great king or a great saint. His father was king of Shakya and Kapilavastu was its capital. Buddha's father tried his best to keep him quite trouble free, far away from daily problems of life.

When he was 29 years old he had a look at four persons. One of them was an old infirm person, one was suffering from disease, one was with withered face and another was a Saint. A thought flashed in his mind – those who are born have disease, troubles, old age and end in death. By that time he was married to Yashodhara and also had a son – Rahul. His father arranged his early marriage simply to distract him from straying to sainthood. But still his mind was always restless to find the way to be trouble free. He gave up the life of luxury and became a saint. He decided that his life was not only for him, it was for all of them who come in his contact. To provide comfort and peace to others was the real purpose of his life. The real meaning of life was to serve people.

Once his cousin Dev Dutt injured one bird and it fell on the ground. Siddharth took it in his hands mercifully. Dev Dutt demanded his prey with the claim that he had shot it down with his arrow. At this Siddharth let out the injured bird from his hands. But the bird again came to him. At this Siddharth said – "The one who saves has greater claim, than the one who destroys."

Whenever he came across any diseased person, he always went in a thoughtful mood – why he was so. Once when he was going for hunting he saw a she-deer which was stammering due to fear of being hunted. He tried his best to aim at it but he failed. The idea came to his mind why the animals are killed? Why one becomes fearful? He always pondered at these thoughts. Once he was riding a chariot in a dense jungle. There he saw a very weak person. He asked his servant – who was he and why was he so weak. The servant told him that he was quite weak due to the disease. Next he saw another person who was bending on his back and was struggling to walk. His servant told him that he was an old man due to which his back had bent. The idea crept into his mind that one had to come to that state come what may. On the third day, he saw many people carrying a dead man for cremation and many of them were crying while walking. The servant told him that at the end of the life, one must die and be cremated. On the fourth day, he saw a saint. His face was glowing and he was quite healthy. His servant told him that he had left his worldly affairs and had turned a saint. At this he decided to achieve that wealth of happiness and during the night he left his palace while his wife and son were sleeping. He went to the forest where he became the disciple of a saint, named Udrak and went into hard meditation. His body turned into a bony skeleton. But his curiosity did not die. At that he left meditation and started pondering over everything.

One day while he was sitting under a tree, he was enlightened and got the knowledge, for which he had left his home. He realised that the wants were the cause of all difficulties and sufferings. If these wants were abandoned then one could be happy. After that he was known as Buddha – knowledgeable – the enlightened and the tree under which he was enlightened became known as Buddha tree. It was in Gaya in Bihar.

An enlightened Siddharth became Buddha and he started preaching. His first discourse was at Sarnath which is near Varanasi. His main teachings are:

Do not do wrong deeds – sins. Do only the noble deeds. To keep one's mind free of evils is the real Dharma.

One should not resort to violence.

One should not do back biting.

Onc should takc purc and vcgctarian food.

In this way, he founded the Bauddhism. He went far and wide to preach Bauddha Dharma. He also opposed the custom of high caste and low caste. Thousands of people adopted Bauddha religion by saying – we are coming under the protection of Buddha. From common people to kings, everybody became his disciple. When king of Magadha became Bauddha, its inhabitants also converted to Bauddha religion and the religion got the protection of the ruler.

Wandering from place to place, he came to Kapilavastu. His father Suddhodana and his wife Yashodhara also adopted Buddhism. His son Rahul also became Bauddha. Gautam Buddha spent forty years in preaching his religion. He founded Bhikkhu Sangha – the union of monks – to carry his message to each door. His son and others went to foreign countries for preaching the tenets of Bauddha religion. Due to such efforts, it spread to Sri Lanka, Myanmar, Thailand, China, Japan, Vietnam, Korea and Singapore etc.

He profounded four cardinal truths:

1. Life is full of sufferings: He saw an old man with his bent back, he saw a sick person. He saw a dead man to be carried for cremation. By all this, he concluded that the each man is born to be in trouble and suffering. One may be happy for some time that too under the illusion of false happiness which lasts only for some time. The wants breed the sufferings. If one is free of wants then one can be free from suffering, otherwise it is not possible.
2. Ignorance is the cause of sufferings: Due to ignorance, the human beings take the sensual happiness as the true happiness. But that happiness does not last long and the sufferings follow. Therefore ignorance is the cause of sufferings. Ignorance breeds greed and that also ends in sufferings.
3. There can be an end to suffering: His third cardinal truth is that these sufferings can be over if one forgives the love for life. That will follow the end of the wants and greed.
4. There is a solution for ending suffering: To end the greed and wants, he found out eight ways, known as eight parts – Asthanga. These eight parts are:
   - (i) To gain the true knowledge: Due to ignorance one's wants and needs increase which causes the sufferings. Therefore the first need is true knowledge.
   - (ii) Strict determination: After acquiring the true knowledge, one must follow that knowledge strictly.
   - (iii) One must speak the truth only: Untruth and bitter truth can also be the cause of sufferings. Therefore, one must tell only the truth and not the bitter truth.
   - (iv) Pure actions: One must act with abstract purity in which there should be non-violence, truth, compassion.
   - (v) Pure livelihood: One must use quite pure ways of earning one's livelihood. It should not be by foul means and one must not earn more than one's needs. There should not be any accumulation.

(vi) Self-control: For the welfare of the self and others, one should always try. Until there is self-control, one does not resort to welfare of the others. Self-control, compassion, mercy are the main pedestals of Bauddha discipline.

(vii) Agile mind: The one who is to speak the truth should keep one's mind quite agile. One should keep in mind the four fundamental tenets of Buddhism and behave accordingly.

(viii) Meditation: To follow the above seven principles, one should have peace of mind. Concentration of mind can take one to meditation form. The one who is able to detract one's mind from worldly affairs, can really go for meditation.

Man can get rid of worldly pains and sufferings if he follows these eight principles.

In Buddha teachings, three aspects are kept in mind – mind, words and actions. The aim of the teachings are:

1. Overall development of the person.
2. Development of the moral behaviour.
3. Cultural Development.
4. Social Development.
5. To achieve Nirvana – ultimate peace.
6. Spiritual Development.

Overall development means development of knowledge, emotional development and the development of pure action. For this the eight principles are taken in view and are truly followed. For moral development the eight principles help the man. These practically help the man to be pure by heart and mind. The moral is the mainstay in Buddha's teachings. The disciples must follow the moral behaviour of the Guru – the teacher. By this way the disciples become morally sound.

For cultural development the importance is given to Indian culture and Bauddha religion preaches and follows it. They had to face the criticism of Vedas and Upanishads, but still Bauddha culture is Indian culture.

Bauddha religion stresses on the social development. For this the man must follow all social norms and must possess all social qualities. This was an essential factor that Buddha helped teachings to spread to foreign countries. In this way Bauddha religion went to many other countries and is the main religion there, despite the fact that it did not flourish too much in the land of its origin.

To achieve ultimate peace is the aim of Buddha preachings and teachings. With which one foregoes anger, greed and the circle of life and death – thus, all the sufferings of the life. And thus, the perpetual happiness follows.

For spiritual development, which is the most important of all the developments, the body and mind must be quite healthy. Healthy mind resides in a healthy body. Therefore the body must be quite healthy. Only then one can possess the healthy ideas and follow the healthy teachings. For spreading the Bauddha religion many devices were set for the preachers.

1. Initially lectures were delivered to spread the teachings of Bauddha religion. All this is what the teachers tell the pupils all about the religion in simple language. This is the most easy and practical way of conveying one's idea to others. The pupil can ask the question and make the things clear.
2. In the Madh (whole time school), pupils remain in the company of Guru, they exactly copy the Guru to acquire all the knowledge the teacher has.
3. The seminars held: Followers sit in small groups and discuss a particular topic by one to one contact. All the misgivings are cleared then and there.
4. Debating is also one of the methods of teaching. One group

puts its own idea and the other puts its own. After a thorough clarification the better one is taken up and inferior one is given up. Therefore for spreading the Bauddha religion, this method was also adopted.

5. Learning by practice: In the syllabus some topics were included which the student knows by self-practising. This method develops the skill of learning.
6. Going from place to place: The Bauddha monks go from place to place and tell the people about the teachings of the Bauddha religion. Gautam Buddha himself adopted this way for his preaching.
7. Remembering by repetition: The learners were given some lessons, they repeat it again and again and thus, these are remembered by heart.
8. Practical use method: The teachings were put to use in the self-life. In this way these teachings become part of one's life and the same can be given to others.
9. The meditation way of preaching: This method was very useful for spreading the teachings of Bauddha religion. In this method there are four stages:

   To peacefully ponder over the cardinal principles of the religion.

   To remove any doubt and adopt only the abstract truth.

   To be away from pleasure and peace and to make the unattached situation of the mind.

   To get full renunciation by detracting from all sensual pleasures.

Thus, the pupils are fully trained for taking ahead the Bauddha religion.

During the Kalinga war so many soldiers were killed from both sides.

At that King Ashoka decided not to wage a war in future. He became the disciple of Gautam Buddha and whole of his kingdom turned to Buddhism. He even sent his son and daughter to other countries for propagating Buddhism. So many other kings and princes became followers of Bauddha religion.

Mahatma Buddha died in 483 BC at Kushinagar. His death is known as Mahanirvana by his followers. It is also a matter of great surprise that the religion founded by him did not take the roots in the area, where it was founded, but it spread to other countries. Dalai Lama of Tibet is still preaching Bauddha, even at the risk of leaving his country and seeking asylum in India.

His son Rahul also adopted the way of his father and remained busy in propagating the preachings of Bauddha religion. It was also great of him that he too abstained the princely life and became a monk.

Indeed, Gautam Buddha was a great soul, whose teachings are followed by millions of people.

Mahavira Swami

MAHAVIRA SWAMI whose name was Vardhamana was the founder of Jain religion. He was born in 599 BC at Kundigram of Vaishali in Bihar (India). His father was Siddhartha and mother was Trishala. His father was the king of Virdhi. Therefore Vardhamana was born as a prince. Before he was born, his mother had 14 dreams in her sleep. During a night, she saw 14 different animals and other articles. Astrologers interpreted these dreams and concluded that the baby to be born would be unique and great. At this the parents were very happy. They say, during the year he was to be born, rain was quite sufficient and timely. Therefore the crops were quite healthy. The fruit trees bore fruits in large quantity. Cows yielded more milk than the usual quantity. In a way everything was more than usual – increased. This was also taken as a good omen. Therefore, the name suggested was Vardhamana – that which brings prosperity.

Once, when Vardhamana was seven years old and was in his school a very deadly poisonous cobra came from somewhere. The teacher was terrified but Vardhamana caught it and threw it away. On that day his teacher gave him another name Mahavira – the great, brave. Once a very learned Brahmana came to his school and wanted his teacher to solve some very difficult grammar questions. The teacher fumbled for some time and could not solve the questions. At this Mahavira, very humbly asked him to let him solve the questions and he did. It is said that person was not a Brahmana but was Indra in the guise of a Brahmana. The teacher took Mahavira as his own teacher from that day – he knows more than him.

To him fields, forests, gardens, pastures, flowers, animals, rivers and hills were of his own self. He used to think that the nature is very beautiful and all the living beings are enjoying it fully well. To aim the arrows at animals is not humanity. Life is dear to all the living beings. If we like to live then these also like to live. We do not want to die, then why would these living beings would like to die. He used to ask his companions, though you can kill thousand elephants yet can you restore an ant to life? The strength does not lie in killing but it is in giving life. It does not lie in taking the joy of others but in providing happiness to others. There was a religious notion that sacrificing the animals in the Yajna open the door for heaven. But Mahavira was totally against it. There is another conception that when a warrior kills the opponents in the battle he goes to heaven and gains the territory and beautiful wives. But Mahavira used to take it not more than like a big fish eating the small fish. He wanted to be above all this and give a life of honour to everyone.

Mahavira used to be in a thoughtful mood. At this his parents were apprehensive that he may leave them in the old age to suffer, in his memory. He gave a word to them that he would not go away from them during their life time. He had respect for his mother as his upper most priorities. Due to the love for his mother he got married to princess Yashoda. He loved her too. He had a daughter Priyadarshana also.

After the death of his parents, he decided to leave home in search of the truth of life. But his elder brother Nandivardhan did not allow him to go for at least two years. Very reluctantly, he passed these two years like a Yogi. The colour of renouncement already fully drenched his inner-self. During this period he persuaded his wife and daughter in favour of his mission – total renunciation and meditation. As soon as the two years passed he left the palace. The town stood with folded hands to give him a respectful departure. But his brother could not restrain him and cried – the palace, for me is like the cremation ground, how can I go therein. In the meanwhile, Mahavira had given a share of his wealth in donation to the desiring people of the kingdom. When he left his palace, he was a penniless monk.

On the first day when he was sitting in meditation, a farmer came there. He had come after ploughing his field. Now, he was to send the cow's milk to his home. But there was no one to take care of the bullocks. He saw Mahavira sitting nearby. He asked him to take care of his bullocks till he comes back. Being in meditation, Mahavira was unaware of all this. After some time, when the farmer came back he did not find his bullocks there – they strayed somewhere. He asked Mahavira about his bullocks. But he, being in meditation, did not reply. The farmer was not aware of all this. He got angry and was ready to whip him. Suddenly a person appeared there and cautioned him and said, "He is Vardhamana, the prince." In the meanwhile Mahavira also came out of meditation. The farmer told him about the incident. At this Mahavira said, "for me thorn and flower are equal. I am not fascinated with the smell of the flower nor feel pain of the thorn." If we think thoughtfully, we shall know that the pains in our account are due to our own actions. Therefore, we should bear them in the same manner. The brave is one who bears the pain in the same manner with which one enjoys the joy. His mind was completely free from attachment, circumspect in his thoughts, words or acts, he moved without wrath, pride, deceit and greed. Like the water in the vessel, he was unattached in the midst of sin. During the course of his travels he visited the pathless country of the Ladhas in Vajrabhumi and in Subbhabhami, here his troubles were endless. The rude natives of the place attacked him and set dogs to bite him. He endured the abusive language of the rustics and bore pain free from desires. When he approached the village, the inhabitants met him on the outskirts and attacked him saying – "get away from here." He was struck with a stick, a fist, a lance and a potsherd. While beating him many cried. Once went into meditation without moving his body. They cut his flesh, tore his hair and covered him with dust. They disturbed him in meditation. But like a hero at the head, of a battle bearing all the hardship he carried on totally undisturbed.

He came to the Ashram of one Tapasvi and sought his permission to stay there during rains. He was busy in his meditation. The hut in which he was living was made of hay and dry straw. The cows used to graze nearby. Due to scanty rains the grass was very poor. One day the hungry cows ate up the dry grass over the hut. But he was unaware. How could he scare them away? When the Tapasvi saw the condition of the hut, he asked him, "why did he not scare away the cows, which destroyed the hut." He simply said, "Whose hut?, Your hut. The hut in which you are living. You should protect your hut."

- "My hut? There is no hut in this world that belongs to me."
- "Where are you living?"
- "I am a Sadhu who has nothing – not even my own body."
- "You must protect your place of living." At this he decided to go away only after fifteen days. He also took vows:
    1. Should not stay at a place where there is no-confidence.
    2. To search a suitable place for meditation
    3. Accept begging and to know the way, you should keep mum.
    4. Only have a begging bowl.
    5. Not to praise and enjoin anyone.

Once, on the way, he was to cross river Ganga. He sat on a boat in which dozens of other persons were there. At the start of the boat, an owl cried a bit. One astrologer out of the passengers apprehended sure danger and left the boat. But the boatman who recognized Mahavira was fully confident of safe passage. It was going very well. But when the boat was midstream there was a very strong storm with lightening. The boatman lost the hope of survival. But Mahavira sat peacefully. The strength of the demon was subdued under the will power of Mahavira.

Mahavira spent 12 years in deep meditation and self-control, which required the most scrupulous observance of the rules concerning eating and drinking. The account of spiritual practices given in the Acharanya Sutra is literally soul stirring.

> "He meditated day and night, undisturbed and unperturbed, avoiding women and giving up the company of householders. He realized singleness. He lodged in workshops, assembling places, shed of straw, lawns, gardens, in cemeteries and burial grounds or at the foot of a tree, whichever shelter was available, he did not care for sleep for the sake of pleasure and slept only for 3 hours for 12.5 years during his spiritual pursuit. In winter, when the cold winds blew he did not seek shelter or burning wood or covered himself with clothes. In the cold season he meditated in the shade and in the summer he exposed himself to the heat."

He would meditate with his eyes fixed on a square space before him of the length of the man or in some other posture without the smallest motion. While meditating he would concentrate on the things above, below or beside. He meditated free from sin and desire, not attached to sounds or colours and never acted carelessly. Being averse to the impressions of senses he spoke very little and was always calm.

He thoroughly knew the earth bodies, water bodies and wind bodies, the lichens seeds and sprouts and comprehended that they are, if narrowly inspected, imbued with life, he avoided all kinds of sins and abstained from all kinds of sinful activities. He did not use the robes of others nor did he eat out of vessel of others. He did not rub his eyes or scratch his body. He had a fixed measure in eating and drinking, he was not desirous of delicious foods nor had a longing for it. For more than a couple of years he led a religious life without using cold water. He completely abstained from treatment. He lived on rough food – rice, pounded Jujube and beans. Sometimes he ate stale food. He accepted the moist, dry or cold food, old beans, old dap, or bad grains – whatever was available. But where there were hungry birds, animals and thirsty beings or beggars standing in his way he would go past that place without begging alms. He kept fast and sometimes ate only the sixth, eighth or twelfth meal, sometimes he did not drink water for half a month, a month or even six months.

In accordance with the rules of the order he wandered about unceasingly, except for four months of the rainy season. During the rest of the year he lived in villages for only a single night and in towns only five nights. He was indifferent to the smell of odour and sweet scent of sandal, to straw and jewel, dirt or gold, pleasure and pain, his world and the world beyond, to life.

After immense sufferings for more than eleven years Mahavira reached Apapa town and stayed in a garden outside the town. A Mahayajna was being performed there. Very famous scholars of Vedas were there. Out of them, eleven scholars were invited to take part in the Mahayajna. All of them were scholars at par and their disciples were with them who were also excellent scholars. They were speaking in Sanskrit language which was not understood by the common people. Outside the town Mahavira also started his discourse in the language of common people – Parkrit. He told them that knowledge is not only for scholars but for the common people, therefore unless they are told about knowledge in the simple language how they can understand it. He told them.

What is a living being and what is a non-living being?

What is the universe and what is the non-universe?

What is Punya and what is sin and hell?

How can one go to heaven?

What is the aim of the man?

Every word spoken by him went straight into their minds.

He added,

The angels may be full of fame and their heaven may be very pleasant they still cannot be greater than human. The angels bow to the real humanity of the human. Therefore one should follow the path of non-violence and truth. For the sake of humanity, all humans are equal. One cannot be great due to ones birth. It is not necessary to be born great that one is born in a high caste, high dynasty or rich family. The essential is pure life and high thinking. Dharma is for the monk and luxuries are for the common persons.

All the living beings wish to live. Death to them is painful. No one wants to die. Therefore, violence in the name of religion, animal sacrifice in the Yajna is a great sin. Therefore, no living being be put to trouble. All should be loved. To make the soul the part of God and to attain perfection these five disciplines be adopted:

1. Non-violence – do not put to trouble, kill but have friendly behaviour.
2. Truth – do not tell the lie, always speak unharmful truth, spread the love.
3. Do not take anyone's article without ones permission.
4. Be celibate and compassionate. The women are not for sexual use. They must be respected.
5. Do not stand on prejudices, do not amass unnecessary wealth. Do not be possessive and greedy.

Whatever you see cannot be the truth. Do not stand on your own viewpoint. Try to understand the point of view of others. Find the truth out of many viewpoints.

This discourse was appreciated in the town and was applauded by all.

After countering many other hurdles he reached his native place – Vaishali. The people came to hear his discourse. A very famous Brahmana of that town also came with his wife Devananda. She looked at the glowing face of Mahavira like that of her own son. She was so emotional that milk trickled out of her breasts. One of his important disciples Inderbhuti Gautam, asked Mahavira – who is this woman? Mahavira replied – she is my mother – I am her son – the milk came out due to love for the son. At that Inderbhuti asked – were you born in the Brahmana caste? Mahavira told – I remained in her womb for 82 days and then I was shifted to the womb of Trishala and then I was born.

At this that woman also became his disciple. Here, the son-in-law of Mahavira, Jamali also became his disciple. Earlier Chandanbala became his disciple and turned Sadhvi – monk. Lakhs of people became his followers. Among them were kings and princes and also scholarly Brahmanas. His discourse being in simple language went straight into the minds of the people. He once said, "Some people breed the he-goat. It is given a good bath and fed with delicacies. It feels quite happy. But the poor creature does not understand the purpose behind all this. When it turns very fat, the same is killed and eaten up. The butcher does not understand the time has come when he would be treated in the same manner. That ignorance put the man in the same situation in which the goat felt happy at the time of good feeding. He also feels happy in the luxurious life." He ultimately said, "You the human beings, live and let others live. No living being be killed, be made slave and put to trouble and teasing."

After living for fifteen years in Vaishali Mahavira reached Koshambi where Chandanbala offered him Bhiksha (food to a beggar) and became his disciple. There a woman, Jayanti, met him after the discourse and asked him:

"Why does life become untolerable?"

"Violence, lie, theft etc, these 18 sins make the life untolerable."

"Is it good to wake or sleep?"

"For some of the living beings sleeping is good and for human beings waking is good."

"How so?"

"For those who do anti-social activities sleeping is good, because others shall live in peace while they sleep."

"That is correct but why is waking good and for whom."

"Those who do good to humanity should wake up because it is good for society."

"Which is good, strong or weak?"

"Both, those who work for the welfare of others should be strong and others should be weak."

When she was satisfied with the answers she also became his follower and turned Sadhvi (monk).

Once Mahavira went to Palaspur. There was a potter. This potter also went to attend his discourse. He liked what Mahavira said. He invited Mahavira to his house. Mahavira went there. The potter was busy in painting the pots. Mahavira asked him the whole process of pot making. Mahavira posed a question to him; will you feel sad if someone breaks this pot.

"Of course, I will not allow somebody to break it."

"Why do you oppose the breaking of the pot?"

"Because I have put in my labour and brain to make it so beautiful."

"Oh, your labour, brain and your skill made it, so you will oppose its breaking."

"It is all the fate which is making it."

"Oh, then why do you protest when someone breaks it. He may be doing it as per fate."

At this the potter fully understood the importance of skill and labour and became his follower.

Udiyan was the king of Sindhu – Shoveer and Vitrbhya Pattan was his capital. The king has heard about Mahavira and therefore wished to see and hear him. Mahavira was at Champa and knowing the sentiments of Udiyan he took way to his kingdom. After passing the deserts he travelled a thousand miles and reached there. The king was overjoyed to see Mahavira Swami there. The king heard him with rapt attention and became his true follower.

Mahavira came to Varanasi. All members of the family of the king there became his follower. A follower of Mahavira, Jandev of Saket town went for his business to Mlechha country. Kirat was the king there. This king heard about Mahavira from this businessman. Jandev also told him that Mahavira ji can provide him the precious jewel. That king came to Mahavira along with Jandev and begged for the most costly jewel. Mahavira asked him which of the two jewels you want – material or spiritual. The king said, the costlier of the two. Mahavira explained both the jewels. The king was so impressed of the spiritual jewel that he became the follower of Mahavira Swami.

It was the year 468 BC, Mahavira was in Pawan town. He was passing his season there. The people there heard that Mahavira would taste the death here. Many scholars and his followers gathered there. The enlightened were happy but the others were deep in sorrow. All heard Mahavira very keenly. Mahavira said that in future the religion would be weaker and injustice would flourish. The selfless people would creep to selfishness. And he was no more. But the people were crying Mahavira cannot die. But it was the truth.

The main teachings of Mahavira Swami are:

Main goal of human being should be to achieve Moksha – salvation to be free from the circle of life and death. To achieve the Moksha one should do the followings:

1. Faith in useful things.
2. Understand right actions fully well.
3. To do right actions.

These are three known jewels in Jain religion.

He also preached five Mahavrat tenets:

1. Not to kill living beings and not be cruel to them.
2. Always speak the truth.
3. Not to commit theft.
4. Not to store wealth and property.
5. To keep control over all sensual limbs.

He left crores of his followers who are carrying on his teachings. Later on the followers divided in two sects – Shvetambara and Digambara. Shvetambara Munis support white strip on the mouth so that the tiniest insect may not go in. They go place to place for preaching and stay at Sthanak. They eat by begging. The Digambara Munis do not wear clothes and they stay in Jain temples.

Mahavira had a daughter Priyadarshana who was married to Jamali. Both initially opposed Mahavira but later on fell in line. Jamali died earlier than Mahavira.

Mahavira Swami will be known to the people till Jain religion is there.

Guru Nanak

NANAK, known as Guru Nanak, was born in 1469 at Talwandi, now known as Nankana Sahib, now in Pakistan. His father was Kalu Rai and mother was Tripta. His father was a revenue clerk – Patwari. He was the first Guru, out of the ten in the Sikh religion. At the age of seven, he was sent for education to Pandit Gopal Ram, who was a good teacher at that time. The teacher started with alphabets but Nanak asked the teacher to tell him the meaning of these alphabets. But the teacher failed to explain the meaning. At that time, Nanak closed his eyes and sung the meaning in tune. The teacher was surprised. The teacher told to his father that he was not in a position to teach him because he speaks like a great person. Therefore, he left the school. His father asked him to take the cattle for grazing. He took the cattle in the crops in the fields of other people. They claimed the compensation of the damaged crops, from his father. He went to the fields with other people to look at the damage. But everybody was surprised to see that the crops were standing unharmed. There was another surprise. Nanak was sleeping in the sun and a cobra was saving his face from the heat of the sun. When everybody went closer, the cobra slipped into its abode.

After this, Nanak preferred loneliness. He started sitting quietly for long time. He had little interest in the worldly affairs. He had a keen desire to meet the God. It was a matter of great concern for the family. They took it as if Nanak was under the spell of a ghost or he was mentally sick. Despite great efforts to know his own position he did not tell anything about all this. His father consulted his family Vaid (doctor). Vaid examined him thoroughly. He advised that he should be taken to Hari Dass who was an expert of insane people. Hari Dass caught his arm to read the pulse and said let me find out the disease. At this Nanak said – "Vaid jee, you yourself are sick, how can you cure me when your own soul is not in peace?" At this Vaid said – "Kalu Rai jee, Nanak has appeared on the earth to emancipate the sufferings of worldly people."

But his father was not sure yet that Nanak would be a great person. He decided to put Nanak in trading. He gave him some money and asked him to do trading. He started for the town. On the way he met some saints who were hungry. He spent the money, given to him by his father for trading, on the food for these saints. By the time, one Bala, had become his companion. They returned to the village. Nanak did not enter the house and stood outside it. Bala told his father, all that had happened. His father asked him – what trading did you do? He replied – he has done the true trading. At this, his angry father slapped him. But his sister intervened and said please do not slap him, because he has come to emancipate the whole world.

His father tried all the worldly methods to detract him but failed. Ultimately he decided to marry him. He was 15-16 years old. He was married to Sulakhni, daughter of Mulla of Batala. She gave birth to two sons – Sri Chand and Lakhmi Das.

His sister Nanaki came to see her father. She talked about the service of Nanak. She took him with her to Sultanpur and he was employed in the service of the Nawab. His two companions Bala and Mardana were with him. He worked during the day but used to sing devotional songs at night. One day working job he was weighing the corn and was counting each charge – one-two-three-thirteen. He carried on but the count did not go beyond thirteen. This was reported to the Nawab – Chieftain. He ordered the checking of the stock. But surprisingly, the stock was found to be OK. But Nanak resigned and said, "Now he will be in the service of God who has given him birth."

Now the desire to meet God enhanced. He took Bala with him and they went to a nearby river. He went deep in the river for bathing. He asked Bala to wait there for him. But Nanak did not return for three days. It was the talk of the town that Nanak has drowned in the river. But Bala was certain about his returning. Nanaki his sister, was also sure that the one who has arrived on the earth for rescuing others, how can he drown. On the third day he came out of the river. They say that Nanak met God and told him all the misdeeds of the people. At this the God asked him to be his representative henceforth.

After this incident Nanak left all the worldly affairs. At that time there were two communities – Hindus and Muslims. But due to the upper hand of Muslims, there was a crisis of confidence between the two. He preached that followers of both the religions are children of one God therefore there should be love between the two. Still the people raised question that you are Hindu therefore how can you speak about the Muslims? At this he sung a couplet about five times Namaz: The first Namaz is to be fair, second is to do good, third is to pray for the good of all, fourth is to be pure by heart and fifth is to praise the Allah.

At this all including the Nawab Kazi of the area were greatly surprised and were influenced by his wisdom. Now was the time to leave the home forever, because the call of the sufferers was attracting him for his real work in the world.

He left for spreading the message he received from the almighty. It was August 1507 and on that day he started from Nankana Sahib (now in Pakistan). He told the family for his long outside stay. But the family was quit reluctant. Still he took Bala and Mardana with him and left for his preachings. During those days there were no facilities for going place to place. There were thick forests and hills. Under the protection of the God he carried on and covered a journey of six thousand miles during eight years. He met the common people, the thieves, the rich people and he went to so many saints, temples, mosques. The main places he visited are – Amenabad, Talamba, Haridwar, Gurakmatha, Ritha Sahib, Banaras, Gaya, Patna, Hajipur, Jabalpur, Jagannath Puri, Singlal Deep; Turumallai, Trichanakalli, Nagapatnam, Cochin, Amarnath, Aurangabad, Dwaraka, Kathiawar, Chittoor, Rangapattnam, Ajmer, Delhi, Panipat, Kurukshetra, Jind, Sirsa. He told the people to follow the truth. When he returned, his parents were very happy. The people flocked to see him. Now he was a saint. He laid the foundation of Kartarpur now in Pakistan. He planned another journey because the Muslim invaders at that time were forcing Hindus to adopt the Muslim religion. Many of the Hindus, accepted Muslim religion. In his view it was wrong. He assured his parents that he would come back and took his two associates Bala and Mardana with him. He went to Vaishno Devi, Pehalgam and Amarnath, the pilgrimage spots of Hindus. At Srinagar he taught true religion to Pandit Brahma Das. He visited Mansarovar, Mount Kailash and Ladakh. He came back via Kargil, Anantnag, Baramulla. The people welcomed him profusely and he was famous as a saint. His main purpose of the long visits was to know more about God. He used to change his clothes as per the dress of the visiting deity – Hindu or Muslim. He saw light of the God in those saints and fakirs. At Pakpattan he met the 11th successor of Baba Farid. He said, the God is there at a temple, mosque or at other religious places, the only requirement is to meet him with pure heart. He went Macca and Medina where Mohammad founded Muslim religion. Some lepers were there at Medina. They say, they were cured when they saw Guru Nanak. At Baghdad singing was prohibited. But when Guru Nanak and Mardana started singing religious sermons, they were appreciated and praised. He told the Peer of that place that there are lakhs of sick and lakhs of underworld. God only knows about him and the human being cannot venture to do that in a correct manner. He went to Iran, Turkistan and Afghanistan. On the way Mardana felt thirsty but there was no water nearby. Guru Nanak removed a stone with his toe and the water came out and Mardana took the water. Wali Qandhari rolled down a heavy stone to harm

Nanak but he stopped it with his toes. The place is known as Panja Sahib. Devotees go there to pay the obeisance. At Amnabad he went to Bhai Laloo. He was very pleased to see Guru jee.

Babar invaded India. Many people were killed. Nanak saw the massacre and said:

> "A person from Khurasan came to terrify India. He does not know his weakness and raided India. The people are groaning due to pain, but he still does not pity."

At this Babar ordered to kill Nanak and put Bhai Laloo in jail. They were put to grind corn in the jail. They say, all the floor grinders operated on their own. Babar fell at his feet and begged pardon. All the convicts in jails were released. Guru Nanak returned to Kartarpur. There was another surprise when Guru Nanak was at Macca and slept at night, the direction of his feet was towards Kaaba, the religious place there. Devotees objected to this, as it meant disrespect to the religious place. Guru Nanak asked them to put him in such a position that his feet may not be towards Kaaba. They removed him to the other direction, but Kaaba also moved in that direction. They tried many times but the result was same. At this Nanak said – "God is everywhere, whichever the direction may be."

He established the preaching centre to carry on his mission for times to come, preaching groups were formed, community kitchens were arranged. He preached for a casteless social order – all are equal at the social level. At an annual fair at Batala he removed all the doubts put forward by the Jogis. He asked them to adopt the way of truth and leave the way of putting the innocent people to wrong direction for their own narrow ends. One Duni Chand from Lahore was feeding Brahmanas at Sarhad (feast for ancestors), Nanak told him that this food would not reach his ancestors, you feed the poor people instead and look after your old parents well. He stressed that one can get real comfort by serving one's living old parents and grandparents. His successor Guru Angad Dev served Guru Nanak very well when he was 69 years old. At this age he felt that the time to go to the God has approached. He started talking little and preferred loneliness. On 22 September 1539 he called his whole family. The other people also came to see him. But no one knew, what is going to happen. He called his disciple Lahna and placed one coconut and five piece. He was asked to bow. He proclaimed, henceforth you will adore, the Guru Gaddi (successors place). Lahna became Guru Angad Dev, Guru Nanak took a white sheet over him and laid. Many people were there. When they removed the sheet body was not there. Instead some fruits were there. They say it shows that Nanak was not physically Nanak but a light of the God, which went to him.

That white sheet was divided into two. One part was taken by Hindus and Muslims took another. Hindus, as per their custom, cremated it in fire and Muslim buried it. The followers built a Gurudwara at Kartarpur. Kartarpur is in Pakistan and is known as Nankana Sahib. He did not leave any aspect of the society which he did not devout to. For this he travelled 38,000 miles on foot – which itself is a record.

All his teachings are in the form of couplets. The Sikh religious book *Guru Granth Sahib* contains 974 out of them. Crores of Sikhs follow his teachings and others also do the same.

As already told, his disciple Lahna succeeded Guru Nanak as Guru Angad Dev and this carried on till the 10th Guru Gobind Singh succeeded the Gaddi of Guru Nanak. Guru Gobind Singh founded Khalsa Panth – now known as Sikh religion, at Anandpur Sahib near Ropar. Henceforth it was decided that no one would succeed Guru Gobind Singh and the religious book *Guru Granth Sahib*, will be the Guru for ever for the Sikhs. Although the 10th Guru of Sikhs founded the Sikh religion as Khalsa Panth but they take Guru Nanak as the founder of their religion. His teaching are not only for Sikhs but to the whole humanity across seven seas. These are very simple and worldly, which can be followed even by a lay man.

Guru Nanak was great because crores of people are following his teachings far and wide. He mainly stressed on being pure by heart and soul and do good to humanity. Even after nearly five hundred years his teachings are very useful to the humanity. These are being carried on through thousands of Gurudwaras throughout India and abroad. The Granthis (priests) are carrying on the message of humanity. In Gurudwaras, devotees are offered food and lodging free of cost, a very important aspect of this religion. His followers have built these Gurudwaras at all the places visited by Guru Nanak to carry on his teachings for the coming generations. He had two sons – Sri Chand and Lakhmi Das – Lakhmi Das had a son Dharam Das.

Abraham Lincoln

ABRAHAM LINCOLN was born on February 5, 1784 in Hampshire County, West Virginia, USA. His father was Thomas Lincoln and mother was Nancy Lincoln. He was born in a log hut and became the President of United States of America and lived in the White House of Washington. Abraham Lincoln was elected neither as Democrat nor as Republican but was elected as a third party candidate. On March 4, 1861, Abraham Lincoln took the oath of office as the 16th President of United States of America. At that time USA was disintegrating on the issue of slavery. People who migrated from Europe to America as Protestants, after Columbus discovered America, were all white and original inhabitants of America were black. White people made them slaves. Abraham Lincoln took the cause of these slaves. Therefore, the white people were very apprehensive of his Presidentship going against them. But he always stood for justice. He took steps to clear the air of suspense. He had moral commitment for the preservation of the whole nation itself despite of the fact that at the time of his election he had no vote in 8 states and still he could secure 40% required votes to be declared as elected. Everyone in America knew that a vote for Lincoln was a vote for civil war in America and sure dissolution of the union. This was no surprise because south had already announced that if Lincoln was in, they were out. The voters of north, to their eternal credit, did not buckle under the threat. Therefore his election as a President of USA was a great event in American history. But that did not look unifying. He had to sneak into Washington in disguise for his 1861 inauguration. He was of course a great man for a great cause and a hero of the time. The time was when a land without slavery was an affront to white dignity. He though, not a very divisive person but he was a great compromiser, to the chagrin of absolutists on all sides and had he lived a bit longer he would have been a great conciliator with the defeated south nation. But as a political figure he was a great example of great uniter.

His rise to greatness came in 1858 during his campaign for a seat in United States senate. During the debates with his opponent Stephen Douglas, the divisive issue of slavery simmered and then boiled over. Lincoln said, "I am not nor ever have been, in favour of bringing about, in any way the social and political equality of the white and the black races, that I am not nor ever been in favour of making voters and jurors of Negroes, nor of qualifying them to hold office, nor to inter-marry, the white people. And in addition to this I will say that there is a great physical difference between the white and black races which I believe will forever forbid the two races to live together on terms of social and political equality. And in as much as they cannot so live, while they do remain together, there must be a position of superior and inferior." He later commented, "The authors of the declaration of independence intended to include all men, but they did not mean to declare all men equal in all respects."

When he took the oath of office of the President, in his inaugural address he said, "I have no purpose directly or indirectly to interfere with the institution of slavery in the states where it exists. I believe I have no inclination to do so." He vowed to follow the Republican party platform and to maintain the rights of the states to provide for slavery inviolate. He further vowed against any invasion of any state nor any use of force against any person anywhere. At the time of his address there were as many slaves in the states in the United States of America than there were in the newly formed confederate states of America. When he was sworn in the office, the states of Virginia, Tennessee, North Carolina and Kentucky had left the union. He declared that his paramount objective was to save the union and not to save slavery. He further said, "if I could save the union without freeing any slave, I would do it and if I could save it by freeing all the slaves I would do it, and if I could save it by freeing some and leaving others alone I would do it also."

Abraham Lincoln is known as a man who proclaimed liberty and justice for all. When it comes down to a President making powerful and life-altering decisions to have impact on entire nation, no man did this better than Lincoln. The best example is the emancipation proclamation which freed the slaves therefore embodying the true spirit of liberty which said, "All men are created equal. The founding fathers may have been great but may not have lived with the philosophy that all men, not just the white men, were created equal and should be treated with same amount of rights and respects." He cared about everyone and for a time his life, was an everyone himself and in his heart he was always one of his people. He shared a similar quality as that of his people "let my people go" spirit. He saw blacks and all minorities as his people. He must have had an order from the God to free the slaves. He had courage to stand firm for what he believed and therefore he set the slaves free. In his time there were so many burning issues in USA like civil war, economic, social and territorial issues. Many lives were lost and many homes were destroyed but he stood tall and proud although he had opposition in both his professional and personal life. Among Lincoln's many challenges included living with and caring for his mentally ill wife. All these took a toll on the great President physically as is evident from his photos, before and after his Presidency. He, nevertheless, succeeded in his mission he was called to do.

Another main factor of his being great is that despite his position in the society he took time to read and even respond to letters he received from the people. The most catching was a letter he received from a little girl to say – she thought he looked better in his beard. That girl was the inspiration to grow that trade mark beard with which he is known even today. He always stood tall both physically and spiritually and was a enormous political figure. He inspired each and everyone and achieved so much despite his humble beginning and great adversity. If it was not Lincoln's emancipation proclamation there would not be Dr Martin Luther King and Barak Obama would not have been the President of USA.

Lincoln had the moral commitment to the preservation of the whole nation. He hid himself in a dingy dusty backroom, upstairs over a store to compose his inaugural address, he started and ended with the oath. At that time South Carolina had already passed its ordinance of secession and celebrated with fireworks on December 20, 1860. Six other deep south states followed. While they were claiming to have seceded, Lincoln, in a kind of secret counter point, was writing that what they were doing was legally nothing that is not void. He began his address by saying: In compliance with custom as old as the government itself, "I appear before you to address you briefly and to take in your presence the oath prescribed by constitution of the United States, to be taken by the President before he enters on the execution of his office."

When he came at the end of his speech, he sharply distinguished his moral situation from that of rebels: "In your hands my dissatisfied fellow countrymen, not in mine, is the momentous issue of Civil War. You have no oath registered in Heaven to destroy the Government, while I shall have the most solemn one to preserve, protect and defend the assault on it. I cannot shriek from the defence of it. You are still in the moral realm of calculation and possibility of better and worse of choice, I will be in the different moral realm of imperative and necessity. I will have a sworn oath, a solemn self-binding promise, you have not. You act differently but I cannot. The moral claim upon me is categorical, on you, hypothetical, for me, imperative for you discretionary. I will take most solemn oath. You will have no such oath. My oath will be registered in Heaven – you have no oath heavenly registration for any purpose of yours. I cannot shrink – you are not prevented from altering your course of action.

He then planned to finish. In the last words he would speak echoing out across the inaugural day crowd and across the nation "with you and not with me, is the solemn question of, shall it be peace or a sword."

When he got to Washington, he changed that ending. He became a bit conciliatory and showed a quite extraordinary literary and rhetorical power of a new sort. But before he would come to the 'mystic chords of memory' and 'better angels of our nature' at the end of the address as he finally give it, there was still sharp distinction between his moral situation and that of his dissatisfied congressmen.

He by his own wisdom not only saved United States of America from disintegration but also brought freedom to slaves. The people who were proclaiming from roof tops that if Lincoln is in then there must be Civil War, had to rethink their position. He took the people in confidence by saying that he had no plan to free the slaves at the cost of the nation. But retraced his position even risking the Civil War on the issue of slavery. He set the ball rolling for the firm union of all the states of the country. It is the path he charted out by which so many other took cudgel of asserting the rights of the down trodden people.

But lifting Lincoln above fray does not remove him out of politics. While political Lincoln may be difficult for us to acknowledge at a time when politics and partisan commitments are widely denigrated, Lincoln's presidency demonstrates that partisanship and political ruthlessness can be used to advance the highest ideals. And there were no cleaner cases than during his 1864 battle for re-election (without which the slave owning South would almost certainly have triumphed) and subsequent efforts to pass the 13th Amendment, which at long last purged slavery from constitution." In the end Lincoln became master of the events because he was the master of politics.

The mythology of Lincoln was too noble for politics began at the moment of his death, with his body sprawled across small bed in a house across Fords Theatre, where he was shot. At the President's last breath, Secretary of War Edwin Stanton famously pronounced, "Now he belongs to the ages." Every age since has invented its Lincoln. Martyred on Good Friday, Lincoln the Christ has rivalled Lincoln the common man and Lincoln the idealist in America's collective imagination. The historical truth reveals one of the most astute professional politicians America has produced. Many of Lincoln's contemporaries viewed him as title more than a provincial hack – 'a vulgar village politician'. But they learned not to underestimate his political abilities. "He was the deepest, closest, the cutest and the most ambitious man American politics produced," observed Mr Fax, his Assistant Secretary of the Navy. "Lincoln was the supreme politician," wrote Charles A Dana, his Assistant Secretary of War, "he understood politics because he understood human nature."

A self-made man transformed himself through relentless political aspiration. In the words of his law partner Herndon, "Politics were his heaven, and his Hades metaphysics." From his first day as a state legislator to as President he was in the middle of the deal making, or what was then called 'logrolling'. Running for legislature at the age of 23, he was unrelenting in his aspiration to higher office. "His ambition was a little engine that knew no rest," said Herndon. Lincoln became the white floor leader in the Illinois Legislature at 27 and was state's leading white politician until he emerged us unifying figure at the founding convention of the Illinois Republican Party in 1856.

Once he reached White House his survival and that of the nation depended on his political skill. Lincoln never believed that politicians were unsavoury creatures, he was compelled to associate with out of unfortunate necessity. He was not a plebeian saint who withheld himself from give and take of the political game, neither did he feel it was a sordid distraction from his higher calling. He loved the relationship of politics, the fraternity friendship and humour. He badgered journalists for gossips they not report. If politics was his heaven, it was also his school. He entered every legislative chamber and saloon, every political gathering and social party, every backroom and court room as a potentially invaluable learning experience. He called them his public opinion baths. There was a title he liked more, especially in the White House, than a late night conversation with group of politicians except perhaps a night at a theatre.

Lincoln knew from experience that great change required a thousand small political acts. Never did he apply his granular political skill more cleverly and effectively than during his re-election campaign and the fight to secure passage of the 13th Amendment. His feat was all the more remarkable for having been set in motion during what looked to be the nidar of his presidency when his re-election seemed almost impossible.

On August 23, 1864 he himself wrote, "This morning as for some days past it seems exceedingly probable that this administration will not be re-elected," then he devised a plan to win the war and save the union during the imagined desperate months of transition to a new administration, since the new President will have secured his election on such ground that he cannot possibly save it afterwards. Alone in his office in the White House, Lincoln folded and glued his note describing the plan and called a cabinet meeting. There he brought out the mysterious piece of paper and instructed each cabinet secretary carefully to sign his name to its back committing them to a future course of action he would not let them read. If Lincoln lost the coming election he expected the confederacy would be recognized as a separate nation. The emancipation proclamation freeing its slaves rescinded and the projected amendment to the Constitution to once and for all abandoned. Hundred of thousands would have been killed and wounded as price of defeat. Lincoln's own personal losses since coming to Washington had been devastating enough. The first Union officer killed in the war, his Springfield Law Clerk Elmer Ellsworth, was shot through the heart after taking down a confederate flag waving above an Alexandria, VA, Tavern. "My boy! My boy," Lincoln cried upon hearing the news. "Was it necessary this sacrifice should be made?" He insisted that Ellsworth's body lay in state in the White House. A few months later, Lincoln's best friend from Illinois Senator Baker was killed in the botched Battle of Ball's Bluff. Then in February 1862, Lincoln's 11 year old son, William Wallace died of typhus. Mary Todd Lincoln sequestered herself in deepest mourning in the upper storey of White House for nearly a year.

Lincoln had begun his re-election year with high hopes of winning the war and enacting the 13th Amendment. In April the Senate voted in favour; neither slavery nor involuntary servitude … shall exist within United States.… Though the House of Representatives fell short of the required two-thirds majority Lincoln was not discouraged. His handling of the emancipation proclamation – waiting to announce it after a military victory. The Battle of Antietam – gave him a blueprint. He understood that he had to bring the public along through events to build momentum for change. He was playing a long game. Lincoln believed that the abolition of slavery required a constitutional amendment and that the proclamation was merely a temporary measure justified by military necessity. The constitution enshrined slavery and Supreme Court had upheld it long before the infamous Dred Scott decision of 1857 that ruled that blacks were so far inferior that they had no rights which the white man was bound to respect. At the convention that nominated him as a candidate – for second term, in June 1864 Lincoln operated behind the scenes, instructing that the 13th Amendment be the subject of keynote address and be treated as keystone of the Republican party platform.

But he knew that such efforts would come to nothing if he lost the election and that he would likely lose if war continued too badly for the north. In Ulysses S Grant, Lincoln had at last found the general-in-chief who would go on to win the war after succession of arrogant, incompetent and dilatory commanders. Yet within six bloody weeks from May 5 to June 12, the Army suffered about 65,000 causalties equivalent today of about 8,80,000 killed and wounded. In a frontal assault on the confederate lines on June 2 at the Battle of Cold Harbor more than 7,000 men who had pinned their names on their backs expecting to be killed, fell in less than 10 minutes. Hospitals overflowed with wounded. One nurse in Washington hospital, Walt Whitman suffered a nervous breakdown. He described the triage in words: "worst cases get little or no attention. We receive them here with their wounds full of worms.... Many of the amputations have to be done over again ... many of the poor afflicted young men are crazy ... it is perhaps a privilege that they are out of their senses." "O years and graves!" Whitman wrote. With the entire army of the Potomac stalled in miles of trenches south of Richmond, Lincoln's advisers believed he was doomed. Running for re-election against former General George B McClellan – the very man Lincoln had trapped to organize the union army in 1861 and whose decisiveness had led to a string of bloody defeats for the north during the crucial opening months of the war – Lincoln was beset on all sides. Peace Democrats, who gained effective control of the party at the convention assailed him as military despot, enemy of liberty and violator of constitution and demanded an immediate end to the war and recognition of confederacy. From the opposite end of the spectrum many abolitionists and radical Republicans scoring Lincoln as an equivocating politician, created a third party. "I would cut-off both hands before doing anything to aid Lincoln's election," declared the prominent abolitionist Wendell Phillips.

Abraham Lincoln won the election resoundingly. A week after his victory, the President called the cabinet meeting and unfurled the folded note that he made his cabinet secretaries to sign the previous August. He read it out for sharing the plan, in the event of a loss at the ballot box, to encourage a victorious McClellan to prosecute and win the war during final lame duck months of Lincoln presidency.

Secretary of State Seward spoke up, one politics to another. And the general would answer you, "yes, yes" and the next day when you saw him again and pressed these views upon him he would say, "yes, yes" and so on forever and would not have done nothing at all.

With this contingency plan rendered superfluous by the outcome of the election Lincoln now made it clear that he intended to use his victory to work for congressional passage of 13th Amendment. The outcome of this culminating act in greatest crisis in the nation's history would depend upon the President's political leadership.

For early help in executing his strategy Lincoln turned to Charles A Dana a former journalist who the President and Secretary of War Stanton often deployed as their personal ears and eyes at the front and for discreet political missions. Now to admit Nevada to the union to guarantee a three-quarters majority which required.

Lincoln called him again, "Dana," said Lincoln, "I am very anxious about this vote. It has to be taken next week. The time is very short. It is going to be great deal closer than I wish it was."

According to Dana, Lincoln mentioned three particular congressmen who might be susceptible to persuasion. "What will they be likely want?," Dana asked. "I do not know," said Lincoln. "It makes no deference though.... Whatever promise you make to them, I will perform."

Two of the congressmen asked to be appointed internal revenue collectors, while the other sought an appointment at New York Custom House. In return for being granted these favours all three threw their weight behind the amendment. "I have always felt," wrote Dana, "that this little piece of side politics was one of the most judicious humane and wise use of executive authority that I have ever assisted in or witnessed."

By January 1865 the effort to pass the amendment was floundering with measure falling 14 votes short. The congressman incharge of the vote Mitchell was the moralizing son of a minister. "You must help us one vote," he begged Lincoln, "Do not you know of a sinner in opposition who is on praying ground?"

Lincoln knew that to abolish slavery once and for all, more and more worldly means than prayers would be required. Congressman James Rollins from Missouri and largest slave owner and an adamant against amendment was sitting at his desk when he received an invitation from Lincoln written in pencil, "Rollins," he wrote, "I have been wanting to talk to you about amendment." Rollins arrived in the White House. Lincoln waxed nostalgic about old political times before beginning his pitch for the amendment. Rollins replied that he had decided to vote for it after the result. Lincoln did not waste time running down a list of undecided congressmen and assigned the work to him for persuading them – "tell them my anxiety." He kept for them, vacant federal judgeship.

The list of favours he paid is very long but he was to get the amendment passed by any means. This was the greatest work of the 19th century though done by corruption, abatement and purest methods. Today the whole world remember him for his courageous work. Millions of slaves were freed and these days one of their man was manning the White House of Washington.

Some consider politics a dirty word. But Lincoln – 16th President was a master of political ruthlessness for the sake of the highest ideals.

John Wilkes Booth killed him while he was President in 1865. His only fault was he worked for liberation of humanity. Due to Lincoln, USA is a united country and dominating the world.

Abraham Lincoln was not great because of the President of USA twice but he was great because being from a humble origin he rose to a highest position at a time when his country was virtually near the doom. He saved it with his wisdom, courage, skill, despite so many high odds. For this he even did not care about his life but gave it so that millions of human beings may live gracefully in that country. The humanity should worship him as demigod.

Karl Marx

KARL MARX was born on 5th May 1818 at Trier in the Rhine province of Prussia. His original name was Carl Heinrich. His father was Heinrich Marx and he was a lawyer. His mother was Henrietta Pressburg. She was a Jew. He called his mother 'angel mother'. His lawyer father owned land, houses and rents that supplemented his income from the lawyer's fees. His father was a wealthy person of his town. Karl Marx received Christian education. During 1834 his club was celebrating the new election of deputies. He was given the honour of offering a toast to King of Prussia, the weak and vacillating Frederick William–III. He therefore, paid a glowing tribute to the King, "to whose magnanimity we are indebted for the first institution of popular representation." He was vociferously applauded and he became the hero of the hour. It means there was nothing revolutionary in his behaviour at an early age.

During school his knowledge of history was defective, he never learnt proper grammar. He was very weak in mathematics and was incapable of solving even the simplest problem accurately. But later on he boasted of having invented a new form of differential calculus. He had uncombed curly hair. His hands and feet were small in relation to his body. Therefore, the general impression was of awkward perniciousness and coarseness. He had decided to be a lawyer. Therefore he was admitted to the school of jurisprudence at the University of Bonn in 1835.

He wrote three essays in which he discusses such a broad variety of serious subjects that they reveal the pattern of his mind, which was to remain virtually unchanged throughout his life. On all these subjects – education, free will, dictatorship, the Christian mystery, the purpose of life – he wrote with high seriousness. He was concerned with the ultimate meanings and appears to have been happiest when he was describing the things on the boundaries of thoughts.

His father died in May 1838. Therefore he lost the man who might have put order and discipline in his life. He was free of parental control. He was free and responsible to no one. He received a small legacy because his father had a large family. He started writing articles in the newspapers and periodicals. He wrote more on peasants. Consequently, some of the periodicals were banned. There were protests and violent attacks on the Government of Russia. He protested to the King of Prussia. The newspaper *Rheinische Zeitung* was banned. At that times he was the editor of the newspaper. He resigned but he had the taste of public power and it had turned his mind away from liberalism to a harsher way of looking at the world. Free from newspaper duty, he remained busy in studies which brought him closer to communism. The iron had entered his soul. An artist drew a picture of Marx as Prometheus chained to his printing press, while an eagle representing the King of Prussia tears at his liver. Marx stands with his head unbowed beside the Rhine, naked except a pair of close fitting drawers. Here the people saw him as a real man.

He discussed with his friend, Arnold Ruge, the possibility of publishing a new magazine in book-form in another country to avoid censorship. He saw himself as an editor and a remorseless critic of the society. He was ready to display this talent of a journalist till the end of his life instead of a social philosopher. His finances were in crisis – he was penniless, living on loans from the friends. His mother even cut-off the small allowances he was receiving. He was brooding bitterly over his fate, irritated beyond measure by his mothers attitude towards him. The break with her was now virtually complete. How he survived during the following months is a mystery because his reliable friend Westphalia had died. He had not married Jenny who was living with him but after the death of her father she moved to her mother and she no longer saw him except during his rare visits. Jenny was in deep love with him but there was question of survival of both. In March 1843 he paid a hurried visit to her and they decided to marry. The wedding took place in the Protestant church at Kreuznach on June 19, 1843. His relatives were absent. He had no practical sense about money. All through their lives they showed an astonishing disregard for its value and its proper use. Money was a subject they did not understand.

Marx started to deprive Jews of their faith so that they may enter into common life of the state as atheists or non-Jews. He argued that the Jewish problem was merely an aspect of the social problem convulsing the age which can be cured once the socialist state was brought into existence. Marx's laboured attempt to invalidate Judaism was neither rewarding nor successful. Marx himself regarded the work with utmost seriousness and employed all his logic and vehement oratory in attacking Judaism as though it was a cancer growing within state. Given his assumption that capitalism, represented by the rich Jewish merchants was the principal enemy of human society, the argument proceeds with a brilliant display of reasoning. He always counselled for prosecution, taking pleasure in his own brilliance as he watched his victim shrinking in terror, and it seems that it never occurred to him that the victim might one day parry his terrible thrusts. He once said, "Judaism is the vulgar practical application of Christianity." He also said, "All religions are unreasonable and have no place in human life."

Marx starts to speak in a simple way about the total loss of humanity capable of redeeming itself only by total redemption of humanity and he will grant the proletariat completely arbitrary powers. For the first time he performs the magic shell which conjures up the proletariat and its ultimate dissolution. He asks what is the real possibility of bringing about revolution in Germany. He announces his theory of proletariat. The proletariat comes as a redeemer. The dissolution of the classes. The redeemer does not come in a fiery chariot, he said. It is not visible but remains invisible, concealed in philosophical robes.

In 1843 he went to Paris and met Heine through Moses Hess. Heine had written many poems against the government. He had written some satiric articles against the Prussian Government. For all these reasons Marx wanted to meet him. Both were complementary to each other. He was moving in the society of revolutionary exiles, sharpening his mind on the opinions and obsession of others. He also met elegant Pavel Annenkov and Mikhail Bakunin who went on to became his adversaries. All of them were of such dominating character that one wonders how they did not come to blows within five minutes of conversation. While Bakunin was a grand revolutionary, Marx was a learned Pundit of revolution who knew all the answers even before the questions were put. Bakunin was living dangerously but Marx had no appetite for such living. He thought dangerously on the edge of thought, beyond the categories of good and civil. Marx was happy to be in Paris. But the King of Prussia wrote to Paris authorities to smoke out the revolutionaries from there. At that time, Marx wrote an article in which he painted as black as possible: The English worker at his treadmill, the Irishman gasping for potatoes, the labourer reduced to a mindless child by pressures of poverty and a suffocating civilization. He even wrote: The private property must be abolished because it is driven from the alienated man, alienated labour and alienated life. Man should labour freely so that he rises to the fullness of creativity, free to live in all his individuality, man should labour freely, not for payment, not by demands of merciless capital.

He completed his famous essay, 'Economic and Philosophical Manuscripts' which was central to the long argument which Marx maintained with the world. He rarely spoke about alienation again because it was of immense complexity and it involved his personal feelings. But it is precisely this sense of alienation which underlines his natural work like a ground swell, giving passion and dimension to his demand for a revolutionary change in society. Long before industrial society reduced men to statistics, he was examining the disproportion between man's desire for freedom and industry's power to enslave. He came to no hopeful conclusion, for he was never able to explain how the abolition of private property would give man the freedom he desired for, if all the property became the property of the state, who would protect man from the state.

In September he completed these essays. Friedrich Engels who was converted to communism by Moses Hess came to visit him. They met briefly. Engels was appalled by his dogmatic tone and at that time made no efforts to continue the acquaintance. But they found that they shared a common purpose and common attitude towards the world. Their friendship began in August 1944 and it endured till Marx's death – for forty years. In January 1845 Marx was ordered to go out of France. Ruge and Bernays, Heine and Bakunin went with him. He went to Brussels.

He played the game of hide and seek for many months to avoid the police. He finally settled at Rue Pacheco in the working class district. Here he started writing. Critique of politics and political economy, but he could not complete it. Instead he wrote his famous book *Theses on Feuerbach* in which he continued the argument he had pursued in *Economic and Philosophic Manuscripts of 1844* to their logical conclusions. According to Engels, these paragraphs constituted the seed of Marxist communism. He wrote: "The essence of man is not an abstraction inherent in each particular individual. His real nature is the ensemble of social relations. The philosophers have only interpreted the world in different ways. The point is to change it."

In that work he also wrote – "All social life is essentially practical. All the mysteries which lead theory towards mysticism find their rational solution in human practice and in understanding of this practice."

The highest form of contemplative materialism – that materialism which does not conceive sensuous existence as practical activity is the contemplation of isolated individuals and of bourgeois society.

The stand point of the old materials is bourgeois society the stand point of the new materialism is human society or social humanity.

His views at that time were tentative. He thought that the nature of the society will come out after the revolution.

During Spring of 1846 Marx formed Communist League with 18 members. Such was the group of 18 which Marx gathered around him in Brussels, arming his followers with a theory and discipline which was conquer half the world later.

At the time of the second conference of the Communist League a document was presented in which 25 questions were answered. The first question was:

Question: What is communism?

Answer: Communism is the doctrine of conditions for emancipation of the proletariat.

Question: What is proletariat?

Answer: The proletariat is that class of society which entirely depends for its means of livelihood on the sale of its labour and not on the profits derived from any capital: Whose weal and woe, whose life and death, whose whole existence depend on the demand for labour. The proletariat is a word for working class of nineteenth century. And so on....

Later on the following manifesto was drawn:

1. Expropriation of property in land and application of all rents of land to public purposes.
2. A heavy progressive or graduated Income Tax.
3. Abolition of all rights of inheritance.
4. Confiscation of all property of all emigrants and rebels.

5. Centralization of credit in the hands of state.
6. Centralisation of means of transport in the hands of state.
7. Increase factories and means of production owned by state.
8. Universal and equal obligation to work.
9. Agriculture and industries distinction be over.
10. Free education of all children.

What is clear is that Marx had not thought out the nature of the communist state in any considerable detail. His own prejudices and ten steps had little relation to theorctical ideas he had already advanced. Some ideas were simply to fill the gap. He was interested only in abolition and destruction. The communist manifesto was only a gauntlet he threw at the world.

In Belgium the government was determined to rid out of storm. Marx got 6,000 gold francs out of the property of his father and he gave it to the fund meant for arming the Belgium workman. At the same time he was invited in France by a member of the government being a friend of freedom. At the same time Belgian authorities decided to get rid of him. The police caught him with his wife with a warrant of arrest. They were bundled out of the country to France. In Paris, the revolutionary fever was dying away. The people here lost interest in revolution. Therefore he saw the hope in Germany. He set-up an office in Cologne and he once again dominated the communist movement. He started his newspaper *Rheinische Zeitung* from here. He was put on trial here also but was acquitted. His newspaper turned bankrupt and he was in great financial difficulty. At the same time, there were uprisings in the Rhineland and the authorities acceded to expel him. He sold the press and paid the dues. He went to Frankfurt. He was sentenced to a month's imprisonment. He was arrested on his way to Paris. The soldiers brought him to Darmstadt. He was in a danger to be shot out of hand. But Marx succeeded to persuade them to send him to Frankfurt. Later he went to Paris.

In Paris, police was in his search. But he lived in Pseudonym – Ramboza. Here he was frustrated a bit. All doors of his earnings were tightly closed and his wife was seriously ill. His friend Engels promised him some financial help. Unfortunately he was caught by the police. He even suspected that they were after him murdering. He therefore left France and shifted to London. He, for rest of his life remained there. He already knew that there cannot be any revolution in England therefore he only saw intense poverty, miseries, quarrels and dubious obscurity. He would see his children dying before his eyes and his wife drawing close to the verge of madness.

It was the summer of 1849 when he came to London. He found a tide of revolution but not that of his dreams. It was an industrial revolution. Here he made every effort to raise money but utterly failed. He owed his landlord 5 pounds. The landlord decided to evict the family with four children and take possession of beds, linen, clothes, baby cradle and even the better toys of the girls. The bailiffs came into the room and said that unless full rent was paid within two hours everything would be removed. It was bitterly cold and Jenny was out of her mind. It occurred to her that she would have to spend the night outside on the bare floor. But the bailiffs retreated for a night. Marx went to search for an alternative, no one agreed after hearing the four children. A friend came to his rescue and paid their dues and they spent the night there. They sold everything and shifted to a German hotel but knowing about the revolution no one thought fit to help him. Pressed with too much of poverty he shifted to a house in Dean Street. He lived like a philosopher in a hideous room with the threat of bailiff always present, with an invalid wife and ailing children. He did much of the research for *Das Kapital*. He used to write articles for *New-York Daily Tribune*. From here he sent a stream of begging letters to his friend Engels in Manchester and relatives in Holland and Germany. A police spy whose secret report about Marx came to light in 1921 wrote about him:

> Marx is of a mid height. Although in the prime of his life but has gone grey. In private life he is extremely disorderly and a bad host.

> He leads a real gypsy existence. Washing, grooming and changing his linen are things he rarely does and he is often drunk. He remains idle for days together and he does work for weeks when he has. No fixed time to go to sleep and waking up. He often stays up all the night and then lies down fully clothed on a sofa at midday and sleeps till evening untroubled by the whole world coming and going through the room. His wife, though sister of a Prussian Minister, was learnt to live in poverty. Marx lives in one of the worst and cheapest quarters of London where there is no clean piece of furniture. Everything is broken and tattered and torn with half an inch of dirt over everything and the greatest disorder everywhere. When you enter his room smoke and tobacco fumes make your eyes weather so much that for a moment you seem to grope in the dark. Yes, there is a chair with three legs. It is the true life of communist chief.

A French revolutionary leader and former member of the provincial government tells about Marx when he was living at Dean Street:

> "Among the trusted friends, Marx in fact behaves with naturalness and he is at perfect ease."

But another revolutionary Liebknecht under-estimated the complexity of Marx, his mind and behaviour:

> "Marx postured and play acted a good deal. He was the master of the subtle art of flattery and condescension and he knew how to intimate and mislead. He had coarse blunt humour, a vitriolic tongue and profound knowledge of invective and he could stimulate artificial rages at his will. He was a man who wanted power and such men are never immune from poisons of play acting and self-dramatization."

A Prussian police spy tells another version:

> "Marx knew what he was dealing with. Marx was not merely a revolutionary philosopher lost in dreams of catastrophes but he was also actively helping to bring the catastrophes about. Marx,

> undisputedly the most capable and most suitable man to be head and the leader of a conspiracy. He is extraordinarily cunning, crafty and reserved and it is only with difficulty that one can gain access to him, but once he has given a man his trust, he will make himself responsible for his man and defend him through life and death."

Although, above all Marx was a dedicated revolutionary, never happier than when he was plotting the downfall of the kingdoms. His habits were those of the bourgeois and in his private life he was the conventional Victorian husband. He saw himself as the kingpin around which the whole family revolved, his word was the law, he ruled from the Olympian heights and he walked with majestic tread of the typical Victorian pater families. The bearded figure who sat at the head of the table was not a man to be trifled with.

A very interesting story was told by his comrade Liebknecht:

> One day Marx and Liebknecht were riding on Hampstead road in a horse-drawn omnibus. They saw a commotion outside a public house. It was one of the regular stopping places of the omnibus. When a woman began to scream "Murder, Murder." Marx who was always sympathetic to women in distress, jumped down and hurled to the crowd. Liebknecht also came out concerned for Marx than for the crying woman. He tried to hold Marx back. The crowd closed around them and soon Marx who had no idea that he was in great danger began to ask what had happened. A moment later he realized that he had entered into a family quarrel and was about to pay the price demanded of all those who entered into such quarrels. A drunken woman was screaming "Murder" at her husband only because he was taking her home. They had been fighting like scorpions. But the moment they saw the strange looking Marx and his even stronger companion they forgot their quarrel and advanced towards the newcomers. The drunken woman was infuriated by the sight of Marx's shining beard. She grabbed it. The crowd began to shout, "Damned foreigners." Marx was in danger of losing his beard and perhaps his life also.

> The crowd was becoming more turbulent and two Germans were really in danger. They were saved when two strong constables advanced through the crowd and saved them from further molestation. They immediately took the omnibus home. Later Marx was inclined to show more caution before attempting to intervene in the quarrels.

Caution was his watchword. He always obeyed the law, took no part in public demonstrations and always avoided entanglement with officers of the crown. Outwardly he gave the impression of a sedate. A Victorian husband whose most daring escapades consisted of occasional pus crawls. He used to say: "The mind of the criminal has more grandeur and nobility than the wonders of the heavens." He seethed with plans of destroying the European civilization at the roots, for demolishing all governments, for banishing elective offices and reducing democracy to scorns. He was consumed by the rage for destruction and by a passionate desire to elevate the proletariat to its proper place in the sun. But it was only in these chance meetings at public houses that he ever saw the proletariat in action while he dreamed of destruction, he pursued the bourgeois life with unabated pleasure as though he could conceive no other form of life.

He did not however think very often of his role as a revolutionary leader. More and more he was coming to regard himself as a catalytic agent who influenced the struggle merely by his existence. He was the theoretician who moved the universe by his thought sometimes descending from the heights to view the importunities of men. He took shelter in the British Museum. But he could not escape his creditors. The butcher, muluman, baker, grocer, tea vendor and the doctor were all sending bills demanding immediate payments. The doctor who attended his dying son Edgar, made his life intolerable. He decided to shift his residence. His family slipped out of Dean Street and went to Denmark Road very quietly. He himself went to Manchester. But he had to return to London and had to face the same trouble of being hand to mouth. His friend Engels suggested that he should apply to the loan society. He himself sent him 25 pounds and also promised to send 60 pounds in the following months. It was a great relief to him. On the other hand, Engels complimented him for his penetrating mind, his brilliant foresight, his lowering genius. This generated the hope to complete the *Das Kapital*. His another friend Dr Kugelman also offered hope so that Marx is mentally free from the need of food and lodging. At the same time Marx was contemplating to abandon his bourgeois existence and declaring himself bankrupt and avoid the importunately of his creditors.

Long ago, Engels had realised that as long he lived he would have to be his support. Marx could not and would not earn a living. Only once in a life, he applied for a job of Rail Road Clerk. But his application was rejected on the ground of his poor handwriting. If at all he had accepted the job, it is unlikely that he would have tolerated it for long. His friend Engels sold the shares in his father's factory and made sure that an income of 800 pounds a year, out of it he offered a pension of 350 pounds a year to Marx. But his expenses were not less than 500 pounds but he was never in need for 15 years. In 1863 he was struggling for survival, rather his fortunes were at the lowest ebb. From the time of his marriage, poverty had been the thorn in his side. Now he was suffering from boils. He struggled for the last chapter of *Das Kapital*. He withered in agony and cursed the Egyptian plague which had visited him.

Sometime Marx may have felt that the sufferings of job were no greater than his own. He too had seen his body festering, covered with sores and with gaping holes, exuding a stench which drove people away. For more than twenty years of his life he was tormented by these boils and carbuncles which the doctor seemed incapable to cure because if one is cured another was at the place. There was a period of quiescence and other periods when his whole body seemed to break-out in ulcerous sores.

According to the Marxist mythology, history is wholly the product of social and economic forces. The blueprint has already been established; the movements of history follow preordained paths and the careful student can calculate to a hairbreadth the exact course which history will pursue, for the various classes obey unalterable laws and emerge according to the fixed patterns. He was not a historian and there is no reason to believe that history follows the laws invented by Marx.

In his life accidents continually playing its part. His friend Wilhelm Wolff died at Manchester and left him his estate. It was sold and he purchased a house in London and started to live the life a bourgeois otherwise he was at the lowest ebb physically, politically and socially.

It was a matter of chance that an obscure teacher of French language Le Lebez came to see Marx about a conference to be held at St Martin Hall, Long Acre. No one could possibly have guessed that such a simple request would have such momentous consequences. At this conference there was the birth of an International body of trade unions. It was on September 28, 1884. This was summoned by Odger a shoe-maker and President of the all trade unions of London. Here Marx declared: "In all countries of Europe, it has now become a truth demonstrable to every unprejudiced mind and only denied by those whose interest it is to hedge other people in fools paradise, that no improvement of machinery, no appliance of science to production, no contrivances of communication, no new colonies, no new emigration, no opening of markets, no free trade, no to all these things together will do away with miseries of industrious masses but that, on the present false base, every fresh development of productive power of labour must tend to deepen social contrasts and point social antagonism. Death of stratum rose almost to the rank of an institution, during this intoxicating of economical progress in metropolis of British Empire that epoch is marked in the annuls of the world by quickened return, the widening compass and deadlier affects of the social pest called a commercial and industrial crises."

Whenever Marx looked he saw evidence of the crisis which arose out of the obsolete law of demand and supply as instituted by the bourgeoisie which could only end when the working classes took power and managed the economy with social foresight. With shameless approval, mock sympathy or idiotic differences, the ruling classes had watched the Russians devastating the Caucasus and drowning Poland in blood and it was the task of working classes to protest vehemently against. The immense encroachment of that barbarous power the fight for such a policy form part of general struggle for emancipation of the working classes. "The proletarians of all countries unite", Marx gave the call.

Since Marx had drawn up the rules and was the sole interpreter, he was in a powerful position to dominate the society. Now power was at his figures tips. According to Marx, 'The International' was a revolutionary secret society preparing to take over the governments of Europe. He told Engels, "The things are moving and in the next revolution which is perhaps nearer than it seems, we shall have this powerful machinery in our hands. If I were to leave here at this critical hour the whole labour movement which I influence from behind, would fall into very bad hands and go the wrong way." This is the dream he had.

In 1864 he was determined to finish the work of writing *Das Kapital*. He once said, "This book would be the trumpet blast shattering the wall of old Jericho. He would open the way and the revolutionaries would take over." About the book he said, "As for my book I am working twelve hours a day to complete it but poverty does not stop chasing. If at all I have the money, that is if I had more than minus zero for my family and if my book was ready then it would be all the same to me. Whether today or tomorrow I am tossed into potters field, alias went down the drain."

The book was complete in December 1864. He first enjoyed "licking the infant clean after so many birth pangs." But Marx's joy vanished as he had the boils again, on his buttocks which refused to heal and this did not allow him to sit. In May 1865 he had a bit of relief from boils. He took the manuscript to the publisher Otto Meissner at Hamburg and he was able to see the first printed sheet. He was overwhelmed with joy. At this he became confident that he would complete the two more volumes but that was not to be.

Marx died on 14 March 1883. Repeatedly, Marx spoke of the corrupting power of money which turns loyalty into treachery, love into hate, virtue into vice, intellect into imbecility. The evil lay at the heart of the society. The slow poison of gold turned men into slaves or beasts or worse. Like a prophet he saw the world in black and white, good and evil in mortal combat, the blessed and the demanded at each others throats. Ultimately, if one follows his teachings the good would triumph and in the last days after fearful sufferings there would be redemptive for all. Marx was supremely uninterested in reasonable hopes. He looked for miracles and thought he detected miraculous powers in the proletariat. He charged his writings with so much power and energy, so much violence and vituperation that sometimes pages seemed to catch fire. What was enduring in him was not his philosophy and still less was his studies of revolutionary power. What was enduring was the thunder of his voice and his curse on those who had committed a crime on human race by amassing wealth which should be the common property of all. All the rest – the senseless quarrels, the devious stratagems, bigotry and dogmatism, the fierce pride and yearning for power all these fall away. The thunder and the curse remain.

He was a great man because billions of people are following his teaching all over the world. Russia, China, North Korea and so many other countries are his legacy. His book *Das Kapital* is the bible of communists. He had a daughter and a son from his wife Jenny. His son Edgar died at an early age and his three daughters were Jenny (who died few months before his death), Laura and Eleanor.

Vladimir Lenin

VLADIMIR LENIN was born on 22 April 1870. His father was Nikolayevich and his mother was Maria. Lenin was born at Simbirsk, in the Russian Empire. His father was the director of the public schools of his province. When Lenin's father died, he was 16 years old. At that age, he renounced God and became an atheist. He got the gold medal at his school for his exceptional performance. He decided to study law at Kazan State University. He moved into a flat in the city. He began to take interest in the radical activities of his elder brother. He had read the novel *What Is to Be Done* of Chernyshevsky. He began meeting a secretive revolutionary cell run by the militant agrarian socialist Bogoraz. He was also elected the representative of the university unit and began to associate with leftists with the intent on reviving the people, 'Freedom Party', a leftist militant group responsible for assassinating Tsar Alexander–II. On 4 December, he took part in a demonstration demanding the abolition of 1884 statute and the re-legalisation of students societies but was arrested by the police along with 100 other protesters. Accused of being ring leader in the protests, the university expelled him and he was put under police surveillance and exiled to his family's Kokushkino estate. His mother persuaded him to write to the Interior Ministry to allow him to study.

But he was not allowed. They allowed him to move back to Kazan with his mother. There too, he contacted revolutionary MP Chetvergeer and joined his secret political circle. Here, he was introduced to Marxist theory through Karl Marx's study of capitalist economy, *Das Kapital*, a book which exerted a strong influence on him. His mother was worried about his activities and wanted to divert his attention. She purchased an estate so that Lenin would turn to agriculture there. Here, he studied the life of the poor peasants which again would exert strong influence over his views. He remained quite unpopular there. The local peasants stole his farm equipments and livestock and consequently his mother decided to sell the farm.

In September 1859, the Ulyanovs moved to Samara where Lenin made contact with number of dissidents who had been exiled there for their political views. Here he joined Marxism with Sklyarenko. He began to read the works of Russian Marxist Plekhanov, founder of the Black Repartition movement concurring with Plekhanov's arguments that Russia was undoubtedly moving from feudalism to capitalism and therefore Marxist analysis of Russian society was apt. Becoming increasingly sceptical of the usefulness of militant attacks and assassinations he argued against such tactics. Still he made friends among People's Freedom Party, particularly Apollon Shukht.

In May 1890, his mother managed to convince the authorities to allow him to undertake his exams externally at a university of his choice. He chose Saint Petersburg where he secured a first class degree with honours. In 1892 he was employed as a legal assistant for a regional court. Soon after he got another job with a local lawyer NK Khardin. Embroiled primarily in disputes between peasants and artisans, he continued to devote much of his time to radical politics, remaining active in Sklyarenko's groups and formulating his own ideas about Marxism's applicability to Russia. Inspired by Plekhanov's work, Lenin began collecting data on Russian society and its various social classes, using it to support a Marxist interpretation of sceptical development. Hoping to be taken seriously as an intellectual, in 1893 he submitted a paper 'New Economic Development in Peasant Life', to the liberal journal *Russian Thought*. But it was rejected. Eventually it was published in 1927.

Revolutionary Activities

In the autumn of 1893, he moved to Saint Petersburg, capital city of the Russian empire, which was undergoing massive industrialisation. Taking up a job of assistant to a lawyer he joined a clandestine revolutionary cell run by S-I Rodchenko, whose members were students of a technical institute – they were Marxist.

Soon after he became the senior member of the group. He openly debated with well known Theorist VP Vorontsov, author of *The Fate of Capitalism in Russia* where his out-spoken behaviour was specially noted by the police spy. He he also met a sympathiser there who helped him in publishing Marxist literature.

He also entered into a relationship with a fellow Marxist school teacher, Nadezhda 'Nadya' who introduced him to a large number of socialist workers. By the autumn of 1894, he was the leader of the workers who met for two hours on a Sunday to discuss revolutionary socialist ideas. At that time, he also wrote his first political tract *What the 'Friends of the People' Are and How They Fight the Social-Democrats*, based largely on his experience in Samara. Two hundred copies were distributed.

He and Sponti were selected to visit Switzerland to meet Plekhanov who was supportive. Travelling to Zurich, he met and befriended Pavel Axelrod, another member of emancipation labour. Proceeding to Paris he met Paul Lafargue and undertook research in the Paris commune of 1871, which he saw as an early prototype for the proletarian. He also went to Germany and studied for six weeks. Returning to Russia with a stash of illegal revolutionary literature, he travelled to various cities. As he was monitored by police, he was arrested and charged with seditious activities.

Siberian Exile 1895-1900

Imprisoned at the House of Detention in Shpalernaya Street, during initial interrogation, he had denied the charges. But he was refused bail. His fellow revolutionaries were able to smuggle messages to him while he advised a code for playing chess with inmates in the neighbouring cell.

He spent his time in writing, focusing on the role of the working class in what he thought was the coming revolution, believing that the rise of industrial capitalism had led large number of peasants to move to cities, where they became proletariat. He argued that class consciousness would eventually develop, leading the proletariat to rise up in violent revolution against the aristocracy and bourgeoisie, who oppressed them. By July 1896 he had finished the draft of social democratic party and had started work on his book *The Development of Capitalism in Russia*.

Along with his comrades, he was sentenced to 3 years exile in eastern Siberia. It was an opportunity to meet other revolutionaries while imprisoned the Democratic Socialist Movement had been renamed, 'League of Struggle for the Emancipation of Working Class' and workers had taken the senior positions which caused the rift in the movement but gained his cautious support.

There was a strike in Petersburg for working hours of the workers. As a result the hours from 12-13 were reduced to 10½. He had to rethink about the movement. The tsarist government came very heavily on the organisations and use of prisons was made fully. By 1897 there were 3,00,000 Russians in the system and he was one of them. He was exiled in a small village of Siberia. He rented a room in a peasant hut and was on the constant vigil of the police. Many subversives came to meet him.

In May 1998 his partner Nadya also joined him in exile. She was arrested for organizing the strike. They married in a church on July 1898. He started using many pseudonyms and finished writing *The Development of Capitalism in Russia*. He wrote that capitalism is establishing itself in Russia country side, thereby supporting a Marxist analysis of Kussian economic development. Published under the pseudonym of 'Vladimir Lenin' it would later be described by his biographer Robert Service as a 'Tour de force'.

Munich, London and Geneva: 1900-1905

After his exile of 3 years was over, he was banned to return to Saint Petersburg. He settled at Pskov a town near the capital. Along with

Struve, he began to raise money for publishing a newspaper, a new organ of the Marxist movement. He visited Switzerland and Germany and held talks with the leaders of the Marxist movement. On 24 August 1900, a conference of Russian Marxists was held in the Swiss town to discuss the development of the newspaper – *Iskra*.

The newspaper was launched from Munich in which his article was published. This paper used to be smuggled into Russia. It remained most popular for 50 years. When his wife finished her exile, she too went to Munich and became his personal secretary aiding him in production of *Iskra*.

In 1903 he attended the 2nd conference of Russian Social Democratic Labour Party at London where a split developed. The Bolshevik faction was led by him and the Menshevik by Martov. Bolshevik means majority and Menshevik means minority.

In 1905 he returned to Russia. In 1906 he was elected to the Presidium of the RSDLP and shuttled between Finland and Russia, but resumed his exile, in December 1907 after the Tsarist defeat of the revolution and after the scandal of the 1907 Tiflis Bank Robbery up to 1917 revolution, he remained in western Europe. He developed Leninism despite hardships. It was urban Marxism adapted to agrarian Russia reversing Karl Marx's economics. Politics prescription to allow a dynamic revolution led by the vanguard party of professional revolutionaries.

In 1909 he published *Materialism and Empirio-Criticism* which became a philosophic foundation of Marxism Leninism. Through exile he travelled to Europe, participated in socialist activities when Inessa Armand left Russia for Paris, she met him and other exiled Bolsheviks.

In 1914 when the First World War began most of the socialist parties of Europe supported their homeland war efforts. At first he disbelieved such a political fickleness. He opposed the great war because the peasants and workers would be fighting the imperialist war – one that ought to be transformed to an international civil war between classes. In the beginning of the war, Austrians briefly detained him in his town of stay. But on 5 September 1914 he moved to neutral Switzerland, residing first in Bern and then in Zurich. In 1915, at the anti-war conference in Switzerland, he led the Zimmenwald left minority who failed against majority pacifists to achieve the adoption of Lenin's proposition of transforming the imperialist war into a class war. In the next conference (24-30 April 1916) Lenin and the Zimmenwald left, presented a like resolution but the conference concorded only a compromise manifesto.

In the spring of 1916 in Zurich he wrote *Imperialism: The Highest Stage of Capitalism*. In this work, he synthesised previous works on the subject by Karl Kautsky and Hobson and applied them to new circumstances of the world war fought between Germany and British empires which exemplified the imperial capitalist competition which was the thesis of his book. This posited that the merging of banks and industrial cartels gave rise to finance capital -- the basis of imperialism – the zenith of capitalism. This gives rise to monopolies. In his view Russia was being used as a tool by French and British capitalist imperialism.

February 1917 Revolution

In February 1917 popular demonstrations in Russia provoked by the hardships of the war forced Tsar Nicholas–II to abdicate. The monarchy was replaced by an uneasy political relationship between on the one hand a provisional government of parliamentary figures and on the other an array of Soviet Revolutionary Council elected by the workers, soldiers, peasants. He was still in exile in Zurich.

He heard the news when he was in a library, there is a revolution in Russia. Next day there was a propaganda – Spread Out, Rouse New Sections, Awaken Fresh Initiative, Form New Organisations in every stratum and prove to them that peace can return with armed Soviet workers deputies in power.

He was determined to return to Russia but it was not easy in the middle of the war. Switzerland was surrounded by the warring countries and the seas were dominated by Russia's alley, Britain. He considered crossing Germany with a Swedish passport. Anyhow Swiss communists arranged permission for him to go to Russia in a sealed carriage train. He was welcomed by the chairman of Petrograd Soviet. But he turned to the crowd and said imperialistic war is the beginning of civil war throughout Europe. The Socialist revolution has already dawned worldwide – Germany is seething – any day now European capitalism may crash – Sailors Comrades, we have to fight for Socialist revolution, fight until the proletariat win a full victory. Long live the worldwide Socialist revolution.

April Theses

On the train from Switzerland, Lenin had completed his famous thesis *The April Theses*:

1. His programme for the Bolshevik party: In the thesis he argues that Bolshevik should not rest content like almost all other Russian Socialists with the 'Bourgeois February Revolution'. Instead the Bolsheviks should press ahead to a Socialist revolution of the workers and poorest peasants.
2. The specific feature of the present situation in Russia is that the country is passing from the first stage of the revolution which owing to the insufficient class-consciousness and organisation of the proletariat, placed power in the hands of bourgeoisie to its second stage which must place power in the hands of the proletariat.
3. He argued that this Socialist revolution would be achieved by the Soviets taking power from the parliamentary provisional government....

> "No support for provisional Government, not a parliamentary republic – to return to parliamentary republic from Soviets of workings deputies would be a retrograde step – but a republic of Soviets of workers, agriculture harbours and peasants deputies throughout the country from top to bottom."

To achieve this he argued, the Bolshevik's immediate task was to campaign diligently among the Russian people to persuade them of the need of Soviet power.

4. Recognition of the fact that in most of the Soviets of the workers, deputies our party is in minority, so far a small minority … and that therefore our task is as long as this government yields to this influence of the bourgeoisie, to present a patient, systematic and persistent explanation of the errors of their tactics and explanation especially adapted to the practical needs of the masses.

The April thesis was more radical than virtually anything Lenin's fellow revolutionaries had heard previously Bolshevik policy had been like that the Mensheviks in this respect: That Russia was ready only for bourgeois not Socialist revolution. When he presented this thesis to a joint Russian Social Democratic Labour Party meeting, he was booed by the Mensheviks. These were called the 'ravings of a mad man'. Of the Bolsheviks only Kollontai supported it. Through his study of worldwide politics and economics, he came to the view that Russian politics in international perspective. In the condition of the First World War, he believed that, although Russian capitalism is underdeveloped, a Socialist revolution in Russia, could spark revolution in more advanced nations of Europe which could then help Russia achieve economic and social development. They said, Lenin made his revolution not for Russia but for Europe and he still expected that in Russia preliminary revolution to be eclipsed when the international revolution took place. He did not invent the iron curtain. But it was against him by anti-revolutionary powers of Europe.

In this way he moved away from the previous Bolshevik policy of pursuing only bourgeois revolution in Russia and towards the position of his fellow Russian revolutionary Leon Trotsky and his theory of permanent revolution which may have influenced Lenin at this time.

October Revolution

In Petrograd, dissatisfaction with the regime culminated in the spontaneous July days riots by industrial workers and soldiers. After being suppressed these riots were blamed by the government on Lenin and the Bolsheviks. His opponents also accrued him of being the German agent provocateurs.

Even the provisional government arrested the Bolsheviks and outlawed their party prompting Lenin to go into hiding and flee to Finland. In exile again reflecting on July days and its aftermath Lenin was determined to prevent the triumph of counter revolutionary forces and he believed that the provisional government must be thrown by an armed uprising. Meanwhile, he published *The State and Revolution* (1917) proposing government by the Soviets rather than by the parliamentary body.

In late August 1917, while he was in the hiding in Finland, the commander-in-chief of Russian Army sent troops from the front to Petrograd in what appeared to be a army coup attempt against provisional government. Kerensky panicked and turned to the Petrograd Soviet for help, allowing the revolutionaries to organise the workers as red guards to defend Petrograd. The coup petered out.

However, the faith in provisional government had been severely shaken. His slogan since *April Theses* 'All Powers to Soviets', became more plausible, more the provisional government was discredited in the public eyes. The Bolsheviks won majority in the Petrograd Soviet on 31st August and in the Moscow Soviet in September.

In October, Lenin returned from Finland. He directed the provisional government's deposition and storming of the winter palace to realise the Kerensky capitulation that established Bolshevik Government in Russia.

Forming the Government

The October Revolution was peaceful. The revolutionary forces already had *de facto* control of the capital – thanks to the defection of the city garrison. Few troops were there to defend the provisional government in the winter palace. The people carried out their daily work while the Government was actually thrown. Thus, all powers were transferred to the Soviets in a relatively peaceful way. On the evening of the revolution the second Congress of Soviets met the Bolshevik-Left SR majority, in the Smolny Institute in Petrograd. When the left wing Mensheviks Martov proposed an all party Soviet, the idea was not opposed. Next day on the evening of 26 October OS Lenin attended the congress of Soviets. He received a thunderous wave of cheers. A short stocky figure with a big head set down over the shoulders, bald and bulging. Little eyes, a snobbish nose, wide generous mouth, heavy chin, clean and shaven, dressed in shabby clothes, he appeared to the masses.

A strange popular leader purely by virtue of intellect, colourless, humourless, uncompromising and detached but with power of explaining profound ideas in simple terms of analysing a concrete situation and combined with shrewdness, the greatest intellectual audacity.

He said, "We shall now proceed to construct the social order." He proposed a degree of peace to the congress, calling all the belligerent people and their governments to begin immediately negotiations for a just and democratic peace and a decree of land transferring ownership of all land owners, estates and all lands belonging to the crown, monasteries, to peasants Soviets. The congress passed the decree on peace unanimously and on land with one vote in opposition.

Having approved those key Bolshevik policies, the congress of Soviets proceeded to elect Bolsheviks into power as council of people's commissars by enormous majority. The Bolsheviks were offered posts in the councils which the left SRs at first refused but later accepted joining the Bolsheviks in coalition on 12 December. OS Lenin had suggested that Trotsky take the position of chairman of the council – the head of the Soviet Government but he refused on the grounds that his Jewishness would be controversial and he took the post of commissar of foreign affairs instead. Thus Lenin became the head of the Government in Russia.

Trotsky announced the composition of a new Soviet Central Executive Committee with a Bolshevik Majority but places for other parties, which adopt the programme.

Lenin declared in 1920 that communism is Soviet power plus the electrification of entire country modernising Russia into 20th century country.

He said, "we must show the peasants that organisation of industry on the basis of modern advanced technology on electrification, which will provide a link between town and country will put an end to the division between town and country, will make it possible to raise level of culture in the country side and to overcome even in most remote backwardness, ignorance, poverty, disease and barbarism."

He withdrew from the World War. He also shifted the capital from Petrograd to Moscow in March 1918. The anti-Bolsheviks were put in jails. In 1920, the Goelro plan was launched and a universal health plan was set-up.

Establishing the Cheka

Cheka was an extraordinary commission for combating counter revolution and sabotage. The newspapers which criticised the new regime were banned, non-Bolshevik Soviets were also disbanded. Bolshevik's own press was launched *Pravda* (Truth) and *Izvestia* (The news). Even these papers were told not to publish anything against Cheka good communist is also a good Chekist. He also declared that Jews are not bad, the rich Jews are like rich Russians and these Russians foment hatred between different faiths – shame on those who format hatred towards Jews, who foment hatred toward other nations. The rich in all the countries are the enemies of workers. Those oppressed are our brothers.

Failed Assassinations

In January 1918 Lenin was in his automobile after a speech at Petrograd. Fritz Platoon was with him on the back seat. When assassins began shooting, the platoon grabbed Lenin's head and pushed him down. The platoon's hand was covered in blood, having been grazed by the bullet as he was shielding Lenin.

The second event was on 30 August 1918 when the socialist revolutionary Fanny Kaplan approached Lenin after a speech. He was rest foot on running board, and was talking to a woman. Kaplan called to Lenin and when he turned to face her she shot at him three times. The first bullet struck his arm, second his jaw and neck and the third missed wounding the woman he was talking to. He fell down and became unconscious. Fearing in-hospital assassins, Lenin was brought to his Kremlin apartment. The physicians decided against removing bullets lest the surgery endanger his recovery, which proved to be slow.

Pravda publicity ridiculed Fanny Kaplan as a failed assassin. It was told that all was to derail, the Russian revolution but the engine of the locomotive that carries us forward global revolution, had not stopped working.

But the attempt to kill him made him more popular than he was. The people were talking, it would have been a disaster if Lenin had succumbed to the wounds. It turned a fact. He remained a backbone of the new body politic.

Red Terror

In response to Kaplan's failed killing attempt on Lenin and successful assassination of Petrograd China Chief, Urisky, Stalin proposed to Lenin to open mass terror on sympathetic people of the open opposition. The shooting order of 25 Tsarist ministers, civil servants and also 765 white guards were signed in September 1918. Royal family was also finished. Lenin also expanded the power of Cheka in this regard. It is told that 16,000 enemies of the people were put in prisons and as per historians, the orders were to teach the lesson with brutality so that they will not forget for several years. One historian, Orlando Figes estimates that perhaps 8,000 priests and laymen were executed and crushing of revolts in Kronstadt and Tambov in 1921 resulted in tens of thousands of executions. As per a rough estimate, people killed in the Red Terror must have been 50,000 to one million.

Civil War

In 1917, Lenin said that oppressed people had the unconditional right to secede from Russian Empire. However, at the end of Civil War, the USSR annexed Armenia, Georgia and Azerbaijan because the white movement used them as attack bases. To maintain the war-isolated cities, keep the army fed and to avoid economic collapse, the Bolshevik Government established WAR communism by which food was requisitioned from peasantry for little payment which the peasant resisted and reduced the harvests.

The Bolsheviks blamed the Kulla's withholding grain for profits but actually most business was in block. This resulted in civil war between anti-Bolsheviks and Bolsheviks. The army supported the latter and suppressed it with shooting hostages, poison gas, labour camps deportations, yet Lenin increased the requisitioning.

The white and red war persisted for six years. There was a famine in 1921 which killed an estimated five million and foreign military intervention reduced much of Russia to ruin and provoked rebellion against the Bolsheviks. After the March 1921 mutiny, Lenin replaced war communism with new economic policy and successfully rebuilt industry and Agriculture.

Lenin's Retirement and Death

The mental strain of leading a revolution, governing, fighting a Civil War aggravated the physical debilitation, consequent to the wounds from attempted assassination, he even retained a bullet in his neck until a German surgeon removed it on 24 April 1922. He was notable for working almost ceaselessly hours daily, occupied with minor, major or routine matters. When already sick, he remembered that since 1917 he had only rested twice, once while hiding from provisional government and whilst recovering from the Kaplan's failed assassination attempt. When in March 1922 the doctor examined him, they found evidence of neither nervous nor organiser pathology but headaches and fatigue he was advised rest. When he returned to Petersburg in May 1922 he suffered the first strokes which left him unable to speak for weeks and motion in his right side but by June he recovered and resumed normal duty. By August he delivered three long speeches in November. In December 1922 he suffered the stock again. This paralysed him from right side. At that he withdrew from active politics. In March 1923, he suffered third stock which rendered him mute and bed ridden till his death.

After the first stroke he dictated papers to Nadezhda among them was Lenin's Testament, a document partly inspired by the 1922 Georgian affair, which was a conflict about the way in which social and political transformation within constituent republic was to be achieved. It criticized the high ranking communist including Stalin, the General Secretary, the unlimited authority given to him, personal rudeness, roughness and lock of fineness. He advised to remove him. But this was concealed in central committee – whereas he wished it to be read loudly.

Lenin died on 21 January 1924 aged 53 at Moscow. More than 9,00,000 people paid him homage – among them was China's premier Sun Yat-sen.

It was said – through the ages of world history, thousand of leaders and scholars appeared who spoke eloquent words but these remained words. You Lenin, was an exception, you not only spoke and taught us but translated your words in deeds, you created a new country. You showed us the road of joint struggle. You the great man that you are, will live on in memories of the oppressed people through the centuries.

The above said words are enough to say that Lenin was really a great person of the world. He lived for the oppressed people and lived for them – relieving them of their oppression and hardships.

Mao Tse-tung

MAO TSE-TUNG was born on 26 December 1893 in a village Shaoshan in Hunan province of China. His father, Mao Shunsheng, was a very poor peasant but after two years of military service be returned to agriculture and became a money lender and grain merchant. Thus, he became the wealthiest person of his village. His father was a very strict disciplinarian, punishing his four children, for wrong doings. Mother of Mao Tse-tung was Wen Qimei, a Buddhist who tried to temper her husband but his father was irreligious. When Mao Tse-tung was 8 years old he was sent to primary school. When he was 13, he was married to 17 year old Luo but he refused to recognize her as his wife. She died in 1910.

His views were shaped by protests which erupted following famine. He was put to higher primary school at the age of 16 where he was bullied for his appearance and peasant background. In 1911 he shifted to middle school at Changsha which was a hotbed of revolutionaries with wide spread animosity towards absolute monarchy of Emperor Puyi. He learnt socialism from newspapers and joined the Chinese Socialist Party. He joined the rebel army as a soldier to over throw the monarchy, but resigned after six months.

He joined the Normal School of Changsha in 1912 and was influenced by two revolutionaries – Dr Sun Yat-sen and Dr Chen Duxiu. Seeing no use in his son's intellectual pursuits, Mao's father cut-off his allowance and he moved to destitute hostel.

In 1917 he was elected to command the students volunteer army which was to defend the school from the attack of warlords. He left for Peking and secured a job in the university library. He studied Karl Marx and Friedrich Engels which brought him to the understanding of Marxism and to Chinese revolutionary movement. When October Revolution of Russia became a success, Mao came under the influence of Marx and Lenin. He began to write articles and he found that his articles had achieved a level of fame among the revolutionary movement.

When the Communist Party of China was formed in 1921, he set-up the branch. He organized the labour movement against the administration of Hunan's Governor. At the Third congress of the communist party at Shanghai in 1923, he was elected to the party committee and attended KMT congress. He became the director of party's propaganda department. When his activities attracted the attention of the authorities he fled to Canton, in 1925. In May 1925 KMT leader Sun Yat-sen died and was succeeded by rightist Jiang Kai-shek. Mao supported the decision to overthrow the Beiyang Government using National Revolutionary Army. He was successful in waking up the peasants who took up the lands of wealthy land owners. He said, "The revolution is not a dinner party nor an essay, nor a painting, nor a piece of embroidery, it cannot be so refined so leisurely and gentle, so temperate, kind, courteous, restrained and magnanimous. A revolution is an insurrection, an act of violence by which one class overthrows another."

In March 1927 Mao attended 3rd Central Committee of KMT in Wuhan which sought the striping the power of General Jiang and appointed Wang Jingwei as the leader. He took a very active role in discussing the condition of the peasants and defended a set of Regulations for the Repression of Local Bullies and Bad Gentry which advocated the death penalty or life imprisonment for anyone found guilty of counter revolutionary activity, arguing that revolution can not be by peaceful means. A committee of five persons of KMT urged the peasants to refuse to pay the land tax.

Civil War

When General Jiang Kai-shek succeeded in overthrowing the warlords, he turned the heat towards communists. He marched on to Shanghai which was controlled by communist militia. They took him as their friend but he turned the heat on them and massacred 5,000 of them and in Peking, 19 leading communists were killed. That May, tens of thousands of communists were killed and the Jiang army marched to Wuhan but was prevented from taking the city by communist General Ye Ting. The Wuhan Government decided to expel all communists from Kuomintang on 15 July. The communists agreed to raise their own army for battling Jiang and thus the Red Army was founded. One group under General Zhu De was sent to take over Nanchang but was forced to retreat and then to wilderness. When Mao was appointed Commander-in-Chief of Red Army, he led four regiments to undertake the autumn Harvest uprising in Changsha. At that time he composed a poem – "the earliest of his to survive – that was entitled simply Changsha."

His plan was to attack nationalist held city from three directions on September 9 but they soon ran into trouble when his fourth Regiment deserted to join Kuomintang cause attacking the Third Regiment. Despite this Mao army managed to make it to Changsha but the city was heavily defended and he was defeated.

Mao as a Young Revolutionary

The Central committee of the communist party turned against him due to his focus on rural areas instead of urban areas. He was removed from the committee. But he ignored the move. He united five villages as a self-governing state with its own independent government and initiated measures to further the land reforms by supporting the land confiscation from rich landlords who were re-educated and in some cases executed. Still, he pursued moderate approach. He formed a union with two groups of armed bandits led by Yuan Wen and Wang Tso. He collected a force of 1,800 troops. He welcomed others to join proclaiming even the lame, deaf and blind could come in useful for revolutionary struggle. He made rules for his soldiers to follow: Prompt compliance of orders, all the confiscations were to be given to the government, nothing to be confiscated from poor peasants. Thus, he was able to mould his man into a disciplined and efficient force.

He did not obey the wrong order of the control committee and joined Zhu and they both took the Jinggangshan base once again. In January 1929 they both took their army to the South evacuating their base. This weakened the central committee. Despite disagreement with Lei, Mao saw Chinese revolution as the key to world revolution and believed that a communist victory would spark the overthrow of global imperialism and capitalism. By this they disagreed with the official line of Soviet Government and the Comintern official in Moscow desired greater control over the CPC, removing Li from power by calling him to Russia for an inquest into his errors. In turn a group of 28, Soviet educated, 'Chinese Communists' Bolsheviks, were sent to China. Mao disagreed with the arrangement because he believed that they knew very little about China and he soon emerged as their rival. In February 1930 he was down, because his wife and sister were captured and beheaded by KMT General He Jian. After some time he married an 18 year old revolutionary named He Zizhen who would bear him 5 children. Facing internal problems he was accused to be too moderate and thereby anti-revolutionary. In December 1930, there were attempts to overthrow him. But he put down the rebels and 2,000-3,000 were executed and many were tortured. Attempting to defeat the communists, KMT armies adopted a policy of encirclement and annihilation. Mao responded with guerrilla tactics instead of conventional war. The Red Army defeated the first and second encirclement although their commander himself came to the close front. Mao proceeded with the land reforms and started a land verification project which was expanded in 1933. He also increased the participation of women in politics. On 14 October 1934, he was made head of the politburo.

He once more insisted that instead of conventional war the fight will be on the guerrilla line so that the long march to success can be maintained. He also focused on the fight against Japan. He fully gained the confidence of the Chinese people and Kuomintang was renounced.

From Zunyi, Mao led the Red Army to Loushan pass where they faced the armed opposition but were successful in crossing the river. Jiang Kai-shek flew away to consolidate his position but communists successfully outmanoeuvred him and continued northward crossing the river Tatu and took Luding. Then they marched to the mountain ranges around Maanshan before encountering the 50,000 strong Fourth front Army of Zhang. Two forces united and proceeded further to Shaanxi where he would fight the Japanese. Reaching Shaanxi they fought off both Kuomintang and an Islamic cavalry militia before crossing over both the Min Mountain and mount Liupan and reaching the Sahenshi Soviet with the 7-8 thousand survivors of the long March.

Second Sino-Japanese War

Arriving at the Yan'an Soviet during October 1935, Mao's troops settled in Pao An. Remaining there till spring 1936 they developed links with local communities and farmed the land there. They also began literacy programmes. He was now commanding 15,000 soldiers.

Along with Zhu Den and Zhang Guotao he established the North-West Anti-Japanese Red Army University in Yanan through which they trained increasing numbers of new recruits. In January 1937 they began the Anti-Japanese expedition, sending groups of guerrilla fighters, undertake sporadic attacks. In May 1937 a communist conference was held in Yan'an to discuss the situation. This was covered by western reporters and thus Mao came into international attention.

On the long march, Mao's wife got injured from a shrapnel wound to the head and so travelled to Moscow for medical treatment. He divorced her and married an actress Jiang King. He moved to a cave house and spent much of his time reading, tending to his garden and theorizing. He came to believe that Red Army alone was unable to defeat the Japanese and that a communist lead government of national defence should be formed with KMT and other national elements to achieve this goal. Although he was despising Jiang Kai-shek as a traitor to the nation, he sent a telegram on May 5 to Military Council of Nanking National Government proposing military alliance, a course of action advocated by Stalin. Although Jiang intended to ignore his message and continues the Civil War, he was arrested by one of his own generals, Zhang Xueliang.

Zhang forced Jiang to discuss the issue with communists, resulting into the formation of united front with concessions on both the sides, on December 1925. The Japanese had taken both Shanghai and Nanking resulting into Nanking massacre – pushing Kuomintang Government to Chungking. The Japanese's brutality led increasing numbers of Chinese joining the fight with Red Army growing from 50,000 to 500,000. In August 1938 the Red Army formed the new fourth Army and Eight Route Army which were nominally under the command of Jiang's National Revolutionary Army. In August 1940 Red Army initiated the Hundred Regiments campaign, in which 4,00,000 troops attacked the Chinese simultaneously in five provinces. The success resulted in the death of 20,000 Japanese, disruption of railways and loss of coal mines. From his base in Yanan, Mao authored several texts for his troops, including philosophy of revolution which offered an introduction to the Marxist Theory of knowledge protracted warfare which dealt with guerrilla and mobile military tactics and new democracy which laid forward ideas for China's future.

Resuming Civil War 1940-1947

In 1944 the Americans sent a special diplomatic envoy, called the Dixie Mission, to the Communist Party of China. As per the Edwin Moise,

> "Most of the Americans were favourably impressed. The CPC seemed less corrupt, more unified and more vigorous in its resistance to Japan than KMT. The Americans shot down over

North China, ... confirmed to their superiors that CPC was both strong and popular. In the end the contracts with USA developed with CPC led to very little."

After World War II, US continued their military assistance to Jiang Kai-shek and his KMT against the People's Liberation Army led by Mao in the civil war for control of China. Likewise Soviet Union gave quasi-covert support to Mao by their occupation of north-east China which allowed PLA to move in en masse and took large supplies of arms left by Japanese Army.

In 1948, under direct order of Mao, the People's Liberation army starved out Kuomintang forces occupying the city of Changchun. At least 1,60,000 civilians are believed to have perished during the siege, which lasted from June until October. On January 21, 1949 PLA troops laid siege to Chengdu, the last KMT-held city in mainland China and Jiang Kai-shek evacuated from mainland to Taiwan.

Leadership of China

People's Republic of China was established on October 1, 1949. It was the culmination of over two decades of civil and international wars. From 1943 to 1976 Mao was chairman of CPC. During this period he was Mao the chairman and famously announced, "Chinese people have stood up."

He took up residence in Zhongnanhai, a compound next to the forbidden city in Beijing and there he ordered the construction of an indoor swimming pool. Mao's physician Li Zhisui described him as conducting business either in bed or by the side of the pool without any formal wear.

In October 1950 he ordered the People's Army into Korea and fight against the UN forces led by US.

Along with land reform, during which number of landlords and well to do peasants were beaten to death at mass meetings of CPC. The land was given to poor people.

There was also a campaign to suppress the counter revolutionaries which involved public execution targeting mainly former Kuomintang officials, businessmen accused of disturbing the market, former employees of western companies and intellectuals whose loyalty was doubtful. As per Mao's own estimate 7,00,000 people were executed during the years 1949-53. As per policy, one or sometime more landlord in every village was selected for execution in the public. Many people were sent to labour camps reforms. Mao stressed for mass repression for gaining power.

In 1951 Mao initiated the elimination of corruption from urban areas targeting the wealthy capitalists and political opponents. A climate of war terror developed as workers denounced their bosses, spouses turned on their spouses and children turned on their parents. The victims often were humiliated at struggle sessions – a method of intimidating and terrifying people to the maximum. Mao insisted that minor offenders be criticized and reformed by sending to labour camps while the worst among them be shot. However, he gave instruction that no 'cadre' is to be killed but drive opponents to suicide.

After consolidation of power, he launched the first Five Year Plan of 1953-58. It was to end Chinese dependence on agriculture to become a world power. With the assistance of Soviet Union, new industrial plants were set-up and as a result capital increased.

A time came when China was in a position where no help from Soviet Union was needed. A campaign for literacy was launched and subsequently mass industrialization took place. A programme known as Hundred flowers campaign in which he indicated his supported willingness to consider different opinions about how to govern China. At this intellectuals began to oppose his policies and question his leadership. This was tolerated and encouraged. But after few months, the policy was reversed and large numbers of people, say 5,00,000 were persecuted who merely criticized and did not suggest anything worthwhile. They say that hundred flower campaign was only to bring out the hidden opponents and rooting them out. Hundred flowers movement led to the condemnation, silencing and death of many citizens, also linked to Mao's movement, with death toll possibly in the millions.

Great Leap Forward

In January 1958, Mao launched the second Five Year Plan, known as Great Leap Forward, a plan intended as an alternative model for economic growth to the Soviet model focusing on heavy industry that was advocated by others in the party. Under this economic programme, the relatively small agricultural collectives which had been formed to date were rapidly merged into far larger people's communes and many of the peasants were ordered to work on massive infrastructures projects, private food production was banned, live stock and farm implements were brought under collective ownership. There was a famine in China which caused million of deaths. Mao vowed not to eat meat and others also followed. In the beginning, commune members were able to eat for free at the commune canteens. This changed during the famine.

There was a great opposition of this great leap forward because the grain were concealed by farmers and town people got little to eat. Same was the case with steel production in the small scale units. At the Lushan conference in August 1959 several leaders expressed concerns that Great Leap Forward had not been successful as planned. Among the critics was the Defence Minister Peng Dehual. Mao fearing the loss of his position, orchestrated a purge of Peng and his supporters stifling criticism of the Great Leap Forward. Those who reported the correct position of the famine etc were branded rightists therefore a campaign against them was also launched and many peasants were sent to labour camps.

On the international front, the period was dominated by further isolation of China. The Soviet also withdrew the technical support. This step was the beginning of China standing on its own legs. After the death of Stalin in Russia, Mao felt that he himself was the all in all of the communist world.

Partly surrounded by hostile American bases – South Korea, Japan, Taiwan – China was now confronted with new Soviet threat both the internal crises and external threat called extraordinary statesmanship from Mao but as China entered the new decade, the statesmen of the People's Republic were in hostile confrontation with each other. A large conference of the party was called and every point was discussed threadbare. Large number of the delegates expressed agreement that people have suffered to a great extent but Defence Minister Lin staunchly defened Mao. A small period of liberalization followed while Mao and Lin plotted the comeback. The grain were bought from Canada and Australia.

Cultural Revolution

'Destroy the Old World and Forge the New World' posters were issued. Mao was concerned with the nature of post 1959 China. He saw that revolution had replaced the old elite with a new one. He was concerned that those in power were becoming estranged from people. They were supposed to serve them. He believed that a revolution of culture would unseat and unsettle the 'ruling class' and keep China in a state of perpetual revolution which would serve the interest of the majority and not of the tiny elite. Liu Shaoqi and Deng Xiaoping the Chairman and General Secretary had favoured a symbolic position for Mao but Mao launched the cultural revolution in 1966.

During the cultural revolution, schools were closed and young intellectuals from cities were sent to rural areas for re-educating them by the peasants, where they performed the hard labour. This revolution led to the destruction of much of China's traditional cultural heritage and imprisonment of large numbers of Chinese citizens as well as creating general economic and social chaos in the country. This revolution pierced through every part of life. When he was informed of many suicides he commented – Do not save them, we can do without them. It is not bad to beat the bad men. As a result 1,772 persons were beaten to death in 1966, only in Beijing.

In 1971, he made Lin Biao as his next in command. But Lin Biao died in a plane crash – he was fleeing China – he was planning to depose Mao, as they say. They were planning to kill Mao but none succeeded.

In 1969 cultural revolution was over but it continued till his death in 1976. He remained passive as so many factions were busy to take over China after his death.

Mao was a great man of the world because he led China, a country of opium eaters, a world power to be reckoned with. A feudal backwater land was turned into most powerful country in the world. He overthrew the corrupt and backward system of China and dragged it into 20th Century. He improved status of women. He carried out massive reforms improving popular literacy and positively transforming China into a modern society beyond recognition.

Mao's revolutionary tactics continued to be used by insurgents and his political ideology continued to be embraced by many communist organizations around the world. Mao is still revered by communist party and is respected by majority of the mass population of China as a founding father of modern China. He is fully credited for giving the Chinese people dignity and self-respect. He is also credited for raising the average life expectancy from 35 in 1949 to 63 in 1975, bringing unity and stability to a country that had been plagued by civil wars and foreign invasions. It was he who laid the foundation of becoming the global power for a country which was nowhere in the ranking – rather on the reverse side.

In 2008 China opened the Mao Zedong Square to visitors in his home town of central Hunan province to mark the 115th anniversary of his birth.

Mao once said, "Let us imagine how many would die if war breaks out. There are 2.7 billion in the world and a third could be lost – let it be half at the worst. There will still be half left but imperialism would be raised to the ground in the world and whole world would become socialist. After a few years there would be 2.7 billion again." Really, he was a great man of the world.

Swami Vivekananda

VIVEKANANDA (Narendra) was born in 1836, to Bengali parents in India. His father earned lot of money but he spent this before his death. Thus, Vivekananda, his younger brothers and sisters had to face the hardship. He passed BA but could not get any employment. Therefore, he was passing through very difficult situation. Day and night he was pondering what should he do. He could still, not find any solution. During such a disturbing situation he went to Swami Ramakrishna Paramahansa, a well-known Swami of the area and narrated his precarious position. Swamiji thought for a while and said to him, you as a true worshipper of Kali Ma (Goddess of the area), go to her and put your demand to her. I know you have faith in her, therefore, she would fulfil your desire. When a person is passing through such a peculiar situation, he can bow to the lowest ebb. One is not capable of distinguishing between good and bad. The ones thinking about power is nullified and are render to their selfish self.

He went to Kali Ma at midnight for demanding money from her for the food and clothing of his family. He stood with folded hands before the Kali Ma idol. But there was a sudden change. He forgot his demand and uttered – Mother give me knowledge only – I do not need anything else.

He came to his Guru and told him what he did. His Guru sent him to Kali Ma next day also to demand the money. But Vivekananda could not do so and demanded the knowledge again. His Guru sent him to Kali Ma third day also but he failed to demand the riches, instead wished for knowledge from the Kali Ma.

When Vivekananda came first time to Ramakrishna, he was with his friends. He had no respect for Ramakrishna. They simply came to chat with him in a jocular way. Vivekananda who was called Narendra at that time put a question to Ramakrishna – have you seen the God? Ramakrishna said – Yes I have seen the God like I am seeing you here. At this Vivekananda put another question – Can you show the God to others also. He said I can show if one desired so. They say, at this Vivekananda was very much attracted toward Ramakrishna and decided to be his disciple.

After few years, his Guru Ramakrishna enabled him to realize the God. At this Vivekananda decided to meditate at a lonely place. But his Guru had already chalked out a very important programme for him to work for humanity as a whole. He was given a new name – Vivekananda. He said – Vivekananda, what is meditation for? Is it not for your own self? Thereby, is not it the selfishness? Do you want to be selfish? Realising the God does not mean that you chant God God every time. The God does not want his own praise. He wants that we should do some useful work for its children. Therefore, you go out and do work for the welfare of humanity. At this Vivekananda obediently obeyed his Guru and set out for the service of the humanity instead of meditating at some lonely place.

He set his goal to eradicate ignorance from the minds of the common people. He set Ramakrishna Mission and opened its branches in the whole country. The main aim of this mission was to spread the message that the root of all the religions is the same God, therefore there should be no rivalry among the people of different religions. All of us are the children of the same God therefore all of us are the brothers and sisters. Should the brothers and sisters fight? Nay no, we all should live peacefully with love and faith in each other. Thereby, we should carry the message of harmony and affection towards each other.

He always held Indian culture supreme than that of western culture which he thought was not so liberal and broad. He went place to place to spread the Indian culture in its true form. He was not opposed by anyone and thereby he gained strength to carry out his mission. Ramakrishna Mission became the symbol of service to humanity as a whole instead of a particular section of the particular society as in vogue in the country at that time.

In the year 1893 there was a conference of all religions at Chicago in America. Although he was not invited there but somehow he reached there. But it was not possible to register him as the delegate of Hindu religion from India – he being not invited there. Somehow he gained the delegate slip with the help of his host there. Thereby he was enlisted as the speaker. When his turn to speak came he stood up with folded hands. He was in saffron clothes. His face was glowing with charm and energy. Everyone there, was very much impressed with him. He started to address the conference. My dear brothers and sisters. At this there was a thunder of clappings which lasted for minutes. He explained the broadness of Hindu religion and the culture propounded thereby. He was successful in removing the mist already spread against the Hindu religion. He talked of universal brotherhood – 'Vasudhaiva Kutumbakam'. His oratory had great charm. The audience were spell bound. They heard him with rapid attention, with interjecting of warm clappings and thundering applause.

There was a rain of invitations after his address and days deliberations. He went to many places and addressed the small gatherings. He was successful in casting his spell of universal brotherhood and worldwide fellowship.

Address at the Final Session, Chicago

The World's Parliament of Religions has become an accomplished fact, and the merciful Father has helped those who laboured to bring it into existence, and crowned with success their most unselfish labour.

My thanks to those noble souls whose large hearts and love of truth first dreamed this wonderful dream and then realized it. My thanks to the shower of liberal sentiments that has overflowed this platform. My thanks to this enlightened audience for their uniform kindness to me and for their appreciation of every thought that tends to smooth the friction of religions. A few jarring notes were heard from time to time in this harmony. My special thanks to them, for they have, by their striking contrast, made general harmony the sweeter.

Much has been said of the common ground of religious unity. I am not going just now to venture my own theory. But if any one here hopes that this unity will come by the triumph of any one of the religions and the destruction of the others, to him I say, "Brother, yours is an impossible hope." Do I wish that the Christian would become Hindu? God forbid. Do I wish that the Hindu or Buddhist would become Christian? God forbid.

The seed is put in the ground, and earth and air and water are placed around it. Does the seed become the earth, or the air, or the water? No. It becomes a plant. It develops after the law of its own growth, assimilates the air, the earth, and the water, converts them into plant substance, and grows into a plant.

Similar is the case with religion. The Christian is not to become a Hindu or a Buddhist, nor a Hindu or a Buddhist to become a Christian. But each must assimilate the spirit of the others and yet preserve his individuality and grow according to his own law of growth.

If the Parliament of Religions has shown anything to the world, it is this: It has proved to the world that holiness, purity and charity are not the exclusive possessions of any church in the world, and that every system has produced men and women of the most exalted character. In the face of this evidence, if anybody dreams of the exclusive survival of his own religion and the destruction of the others, I pity him from the bottom of my heart, and point out to him that upon the banner of every religion will soon be written in spite of resistance: "Help and not fight," "Assimilation and not Destruction," "Harmony and Peace and not Dissension."

He further said:

"Work incessantly but be not attached to it. The actions can be translated very nearly by inherent tendency. Using the smile of a lake for the mind, every ripple, every wave, that rises in the mind when it subsides does not die entirely, but leaves a mark and a future possibility of that wave coming out again. This mark with the possibility of the wave reappearing is what is called Samsakar. Every work that we do, every movement of the body, every thought that we think, leaves such an impression on the mind, stuff and even when such impression are not obvious on the surface, they are sufficiently strong to work beneath the surface, subconsciously. What we are every movement is determined by the sum total of these impressions on the mind. What I am just at this movement is the effect of the sum total of all the impressions of my past life. This is really what is meant by character, each mans character is determined by the sum totals of the these impressions. If good impressions prevails, the character becomes good, if bad it becomes bad. If a man continuously hears bad words, thinks bad thoughts, does bad actions his mind will be full of bad impressions and they shall influence his thought and work without his being conscious of that fact. In fact these bad impressions are always working and their resultant must be evils and that man will be a bad man, he cannot help it. The sum total of these impressions in him well create the strong motive power for doing bad actions. He will be like a machine in the hands of impression and they will force him to do evil. Similarly, if a man thinks good thoughts and does good work, the sum total of these impressions will be good and they in a similar manner force him to do good work even in spite of himself. When a man has done so much good work and thoughts so many good thoughts that there is an irresistible tendency in him to do good work in spite of himself and even he wishes to do evil, his mind as the sum total of his tendencies will not allow him to do so; the tendencies will turn him back, he is completely under the impression of good tendencies. When such is the case, a man's good character is said to be established.

As the tortoise ducts its feet and the head inside the shell and you may kill it or destroy, it will not come out, even so the character of that man who has control over motives and organs is unchangeably established. He controls his own inner forces and nothing can draw them out against his will. By this continuous reflex of good thoughts, good impressions moving over the surface of the mind, the tendency for doing good becomes strong and as a result, we are able to control sensual organs. Thus, along with the character be established, then alone a man gets to truths. Such a man is safe for ever, he cannot do any evil. You may place him in any company there will be no danger for him. There is still higher state than having this good tendency and that is the desire for liberation. You must remember that the freedom of the soul is the goal of all and each one equally leads to the same result. By work alone, man can get to where Buddha got largely by meditation or Christ by prayer. Buddha was working Ianam, Christ was a Bhahat but the same goal was reached by both of them. The difficulty is here. The liberation means entire freedom – freedom from bondage of good as well as bondage of evils. A golden chain is as much a chain as an iron one. There is a thorn in my finger and I use another to take the first one out and when I have taken it out I throw both of them aside. I have no necessity for keeping a second thorn because both are thorn after all. So the bad tendencies are to be counteracted by the good ones and the bad impressions on the mind should be removed by fresh waves of good ones, until all that is evil almost disappear or is subdued and held in control in a corner of the mind but after that good tendencies have also to be conquered. Thus, the 'attached' becomes the unattached work, but let not the action or thought produce deep impression on the mind. Let the ripples come and go, let huge actions proceed from the muscles and the brain but let them not make any deep impression on the soul.

How can this be done? We see that the impression of any action to which we attach ourselves remains. I may meet hundred of persons during the day and among them meet also, one whom I love and when I retire at night I may try to think of all the faces. I saw, but only that face comes before the mind – the face which I met perhaps only for a minute and which I loved all the others have vanished. My attachment to this particular person caused a deep impression on my mind than all the other faces. Physiologically, the impressions have all been the same, every one of the faces that I saw pictured itself on the retina and the brain took the pictures in, yet there was no similarity of the effect upon the mind. Most of the faces perhaps were entirely new faces, about which I have never thought before, but that one face of which I got only a glimpse found association inside. Perhaps I pictured him in my mind for years knew hundred of things about him and this new vision of him awakened hundred of sleeping memories in my mind and this one impression having been repeated perhaps hundred time more than those of the different faces together will produce a great effect on the mind.

Therefore, you should do work like a master and not like a slave. If you buy a slave and tie him down in chains, make him work for you he will work like a drudge but there will be no love in him. So when we ourselves work for the things of the world as slaves there can be no love in us and work is not true work. This is true of work done for relative and friends and so true of work done for our own selves. Selfish work is slave work and there is a test. Every act of love brings happiness, there is no act of love which does not bring peace and blessedness as its reaction. Real existence, real knowledge and real love are eternally connected with one another, the three in one where one of them is, the others must be, they are three aspects of the one without a second – the existence – knowledge-bliss. One, that existence becomes relative we see it as the world, that knowledge becomes in its turn modified into the knowledge of things of the world and that bliss forms the foundation of all true love known by the heart of the man."

He once said,

> "Helping others physically, by removing their social needs is indeed great, but the help is greater according as the need is greater and according as the help is far reaching. If a man's wants can be removed for an hour, it is helping him indeed; if his wants can be removed for a year it will be more help to him; but if his wants can be removed forever it is surely the greatest help and that can be given to him. Spiritual knowledge is the only thing that can destroy our miseries forever, any knowledge satisfies wants for a time. It is only with the knowledge of spirit that the faculty of want is annihilated forever, so helping a man spiritually is the highest help that can be given to him. He who gives man the spiritual knowledge, is the greatest benefactor of mankind and as such we always find that those were the most powerful men who helped man in his spiritual need, because spirituality is the true basis of all our activities in life. A spiritually strong and sound man will be strong in every other respect, if he so wishes.
>
> The miseries of the world cannot be removed by physical help only. Until the nature of the man changes, these physical needs will always arise and miseries will always be felt and no amount of physical help will cure them completely. The only solution to this problem is to make mankind pure. Ignorance is the mother of all the evils and all the miseries we see. Let man have light and let them be pure and spiritually strong and educated, then alone the misery will cease in the world not before. Charities, asylums and free hospitals can not remove miseries but the character can do it."

Once Vivekananda was talking about future of India. He said:

> "This is the ancient land where wisdom made its home before it went into any other country, The same India whose influx of super spirituality is represented as it were, on the material plane, by rolling rivers like oceans, where the eternal Himalayas, rising tier above tier with their snow caps, look as it were into the very mysteries of heaven. Here is the same India whose soil has been

trodden by the feet of the greatest sages that ever lived. Here first sprang up inquiries into the nature of the man and into the internal world. Here first rose the doctrines of immortality of the soul, the existence of a supervising God, an immanent God in nature and in man, and have the highest ideals of religion and philosophy, have attained their culminating points. This is the land from whence, like the tidal waves, spirituality and philosophy have again and again rushed out and deluged the world and this is the land from whence once more such tides must proceed in order to bring life and vigour into the decaying of races of mankind. It is the same India, which has withstood the shocks of centuries, of hundred of foreign invasions, of hundreds of upheavals of manners and customs. It is the same land which stands firmer than any rock in the world with its undying vigour, indestructible life. Its life is of the same nature as the soul, without beginning and without end, immoral and we are the children of that great country.

The problems in India are more complicated, more momentous than in any other country, race, religion, language and government – all these together make the nation. The elements which compose the nations of the world are indeed very few, taking race after race compared to this country. Here have been the Aryan, Dravidian, Tartar, the Turk, Mongol, European – all the races of the world, as it were, pouring their blood into this land. Of languages, the most wonderful conglomeration is here of manners and customs. There is more difference between the two Indian races than between the European and Eastern races.

The one common ground that we have is our scared traditions. That is the common ground and upon that we shall have to build. In Europe the political ideas form the national unity. The unity in traditions – religion, therefore is absolutely necessary as the first condition of the future of India. There must be recognition of one religion throughout the length and breadth of this land. What do I mean by one religion? Not the sense of one religion as held among the Christians or Mohammedans or the Buddhists. We know that our religion has certain common grounds, commons to all our sects, however varying their conclusions may be, however different their claims may be. So there are certain common grounds and within their limitations, this religion of ours admits of a marvellous variation, an infinite amount of liberty to think and live our own loves. We all know that, at least those of life giving common principles of our religion and let every man woman and child throughout the length and breadth of this country, understand them, know them and try to bring them out in their lives. This is the first step and therefore it has to be taken.

Giving a call to the youths he said:

"My hope is that you will respond to the call of your nation. Each one of you has a glorious future if you dare – believe me. Have tremendous faith in you, like the faith I had when I was a child and which I am working out now. Have that faith, each one of you. That eternal power lodged in every soul – and you will revive the whole of India. Ay, we shall then go to every country under the sun and our Ideas will before long be a component of many forces that are working to make up every nation in the world. We must enter into the life of every race in India and abroad we shall have to work to bring this about. Now for that I want the young men. 'It is the young strong and healthy, of sharp intellect that will reach the lord,' say Vedas. This is the time to decide your future – while you possess the energy of youth not when you are worn out and jaded but in the freshness and vigour of youth. Work, this is the time, for freshest, the untouched and unsmelled flowers alone are to be laid at the feet of the lord and such he receives, Rouse yourselves, therefore, life is short – there are greater works to be done."

He once said to a disciple:

"But saying 'I can do' won't do. Show me through action what you can do and then only I shall know that your coming to me is turned to some good account. Get up and put your shoulder to the wheel –

how long is this life for? As you have come into this world, leave some mark behind. Otherwise where is the difference between you and the trees and stones? They too come into existence, decay and die. If you like to be born and to die like them you are at liberty to do so. Show me by your actions that your actions are fruitful to the highest order. Go and tell all, 'In everyone of you lies the eternal power, try to wake it up.' What will you do with individual salvation? That is sheer selfishness. Throw aside your meditation, throw away your salvation and such things. But your whole heart and soul in the work to which I have consecrated myself.

First of all make the soil ready and thousands of Vivekananda in time will be born into this world to deliver such lectures. You need not worry yourself about that. Don't you see, why I am starting orphanages, famine relief works etc? And can not you being Indian, similarly serve your own people, your country men?

Once he said, Principles exist, we do not create them, we only discover them. Religion consists solely in realization. Doctrines are methods not religion. All the different religions are but application of one religion adapted to suit the requirements of different nations. Theories only lead to fightings; Thus, the name of the God that ought bring peace has been the cause of half the bloodshed of the world. Go to the direct source. Ask God what he is? Unless he answers he is not, he is not, but every religion teaches that he does answer.

Have something to say for yourself, else how can you have any idea of what others have said? Do not cling to old superstitions, be ready for new truths. Fools are they who drink brackish water from a well their forefathers dug and would not drink pure water from a new well that other have dug unless we realize God for ourselves we can know nothing about him. Each man is perfect by nature, prophets have manifested this perfection but it is potential in us. How can we understand that Moses saw God unless we see him? If God came to anyone, he will come to me. I will go to God direct let him talk to me, I can not take, belief as a basis that is atheism and blasphemy. If God spoke to a man in the desert of Arabia two thousand years ago, He can also speak to me today, how can I know that he has not died? Come to God any way you can, only come. But in coming do not push anyone down.

The knowing ones must have pity on ignorants. One who knows is willing to give up his body even for an ant because he knows that body is nothing.

Is it necessary to pass through all the lower stages to reach the highest, or can a plunge be taken at once? The modern American boy takes 25 years to attain that which his forefathers took hundred years to do. Present day, a Hindu gets in twenty years to the height reached in eight thousands years by his ancestors. On the physical side the embryo goes from the amoeba to man in the womb. These are the teachings of the modern science. The time is the only measure of our thoughts and thoughts being inconceivable swift, there is no limit to the speed with which we can live the life ahead. So it cannot be stated how long it would take to live all future life. It might be in a second, or it might take fifty life times. It depends on the intensity of the desire. Teaching must therefore be modified according to the need of the taught."

He once said:

"Go all of you, wherever there is an outbreak of plague or famine, or whenever the people are in distress, mitigate their sufferings. At the most you may die in the attempt what of that. How many like you are being born and dying like worms every day? What difference does it make to the world at large? Die you must but have a great deal to die for and it is better to die with great deal in life. Preach this ideal from door to door and you will yourselves be benefited by it and at the same time that you are doing good to your country. I see extreme pain to see you leading a life of inaction. Set yourselves to work – to work. Do not sit idle, do not tarry – the time of death is approaching day by day. Do not think that everything would be done in time, later on. Mind, nothing will be done that way."

Before he died in 1902 he prepared thousands of young persons to work for humanity. He started the mission in the name of his Guru Ramakrishna. These centres of practical work are working throughout the country and abroad, without any selfish motto. That is the work for humanity. The people are appreciating that work. And in that work, Swami Vivekananda is still lives to fulfil the word he gave to his Guru – "do not be selfish, do concrete work for humanity." Really like other great persons, the humanity is benefited by the birth of Narendra Swami Vivekananda.

Nutshell of Vivekananda's Teachings

Each soul is potentially divine. The goal is to manifest this divinity within, by controlling nature, external and internal Do this either by work or worship, or psychic control, or philosophy – by one or more or all these – and be free. This is the whole religion, doctrines or dogmas or rituals, or books or temples, or forms, are but secondary details.

At the World's Parliament of Religions, Chicago, Vivekananda said about the different religions:

> "As the different streams having their different resources in different places all mingle their water in the sea, so Oh, Lord, different paths which men take through different tendencies, various though they appear crooked or straight, all lead to these. His disciple sister Christine said about him:
>
> He was a radiant being, who had descended from another, from a high sphere for a definite purpose. One might have known that he would not stay long it is to be wondered at that nature itself rejoices in such a birth that the heavens open and the angels sing paeans of praise?
>
> Blessed is the country in which he was born, blessed are they who lived on this earth at the same time and blessed thrice are the few who sat at his feet."

Since he was a bachelor, therefore, question of offspring does not arise.

Swami Dayananda Saraswati

DAYANANDA was born in village Tankara near Morbi in Rajkot district of Gujarat province of India in the year 1824. His original name was Mool Shankar. His father was Karshanji Lalji Tiwari and his mother was Yashodabai. His parents were Hindu Brahmanas. They were worshippers of Hindu Devatas (Gods). Once, when he was not an adult, a Hindu religious festival Shivaratri was being celebrated in the village temple. Shiva's devotees gathered there and devotional songs were sung and sermons were given. At about midnight, the singing of the songs with the beat of the drum stopped. Almost all present there fell asleep. The young Mool Shankar did not sleep. A mouse, came from somewhere and started playing on the idol of the Shivaji in the temple. During the sermons by the priests he had heard – Shivaji was all powerful. An idea came to the mind of this young boy – when Shivaji is all powerful then why a creature like a mouse is playing on it. Even this small creature is not aware of the power of this god. He thought over this again and again but could reach a conclusion that, the idol is powerless and its worship is all futile. All those devotees here are under the false spell – with wrong a notion.

Dayananda took a vow to remain Brahmachari (celibate) and to spread the knowledge of the Vedas to the public in general, in true spirit. But the people of Sanatana Dharma were fully alarmed of his move which was an assault on their loaves and fish which were enjoyed with the help of myths and fake preachings. Dayananda invited them for debates. Some came and other did not. The people were impressed by his views and therefore took interest in following his teachings. But these teachings were like a red rag to a bull to those who had been exploiting the people by the dint of their concocted tenets. Therefore, he had to face the staunch opposition from these elements which were well entrenched in their profession to misguide the general public for their narrow ends. Dayananda had many unsavoury encounters with these elements.

Because the people, generation after generation were following the misguided norms fixed by the semi literate Brahmanas therefore. these were fully embedded in the minds of the public in general. This was proving very hard for convincing the people to rationality. Therefore, Dayananda had to face very stiff opposition everywhere in the country. Even the holy book of the Hindus – Vedas – were distorted in the favour of those who were perpetuating the idolity. The deaths of his younger sister and uncle from cholera caused Dayananda to ponder the meaning of life and death and he started asking the questions which worried his parents. He was to be married in his early teens, as was common those days. But he ran away from home in 1946.

He left home in search of true knowledge. He went to various places in jungles and mountains as an ascetic for 25 years up to 1869 but he was not satisfied with the reasoning and arguments propounded by the so called scholars. Finally, he came to Mathura in Uttar Pardesh, India. There was a blind saint Virjanand who believed, that the Hindus had strayed in darkness and had become impure. Dayananda came in his contact. He found his teachings free from myths. Therefore, he decided to stay with him in his small kutia (hut). There he learnt the Vedas which are full of true knowledge for the mankind. He devotedly followed the teachings of the Vedas. He remained there for many years.

Thereby, he could gather the full and true knowledge of Vedas. Vedas do not call for the blind following like the other Hindu religion scriptures puranas and shastras. In Vedas there is no idol worship but the only worship of God who is omnipresent, omnipotent and omniscient. Swami Virjanand taught him what the early Aryans used to know and follow. In that knowledge, there was no place for exploitation on the strength of myths and false notions. All were free from the trace of the blind following in the guise of idol worships. Mool Shankar followed celibacy and acquired the knowledge he cherished. When Guru (teacher) Swami Virjanand was fully satisfied with, not only the knowledge his disciple acquired but also the capacity with which he can cast the spell of his knowledge on others, then he asked the disciple to go out to spread the teachings of Vedas. He also gave him the new name – Dayananda.

Dayananda carried on steadfastly and did not lose hope in the task given by his Guru Swami Virjanand. To remove the darkness from the minds of those who took the religious teachings as a holy cow, proved a very hard nut to crack. After few years he was successful to persuade hundred or so rational persons to his teachings.

He gathered them at Bombay in the year 1875 and formed a new social society known as Arya Samaj. Arya means the best among the people and Samaj means society. This simply means the organization of the best persons. He with the help of these people, fully encouraged, travelled through out the country for spreading, the message of Arya Samaj. Branches of Arya Samaj were established in all the provinces of the country. These branches took the task to the villages with help of devoted singers and preaches. After a decade, the influence of Arya Samaj was visible. There was enough literature for distribution among the public in general. Dayananda's mission was not to start a new religion or sect but to tell the humankind about the universal brotherhood through nobility as spelt out in Vedas. For that mission, Arya Samaj was founded enunciating the ten universal principles as code for universalism Krinvanto Vishwaryam, meaning, the whole world be the abode for nobles (Aryas). His next step was to take the difficult task of reforming Hinduism with dedication, despite multiple repeated attempts on his personal life. He travelled on the strength of his arguments based on his knowledge of Sanskrit language and Vedas. He believed that Hinduism had been corrupted by divergence from the founding principles of Vedas and that Hindus had been misled by the priesthood for the priests, self-aggrandizement. Hindu priests discouraged the lay man from reading the Vedas and encouraged the rituals such on bathing in Ganga river and feeding of priests on anniversaries which Dayananda pronounced as superstitions or self-serving practices. By exerting the nation to reject such superstitious notions, his aim was to educate the nation and to go back to Vedas. He wanted the people who followed Hinduism to go back to the roots and follow the Vedic life which he pointed out. He exerted the Hindus to accept the social reforms like the abolition of untouchability, Sati and dowry, education of women, Swadeshi and importance of cows for national prosperity as well as the adoption of Hindi as a national language for national integration. Through his daily life and practices of yoga and Asanas, teachings and preachings, sermons and writings, he inspired the Hindus to aspire Swarajya (self-government) nationalism and spiritualism. He advocated equal rights for women and education of girls. He did logical, scientific and critical analysis of all faiths i.e. Christianity, Jainism, Buddhism and Sikhism, but he did not criticize Islam. In addition to denouncing idolatry in Hinduism, as may be seen in his book *Satyaratha Prakasha* he was against what he considered to be corruption of true and pure faith in his own country. Unlike many other reform movements of his times within Hinduism the Arya Samaj's appeal was addressed not only to the educated few in India but to the world as evidenced in the Sixth principle of Arya Samaj. His teachings were for all and not for a sect, faith or community.

He said that accept Dharma – religion, whatever is in full conformity with impartial justice, truthfulness and the like; that which is not opposed to teachings of God as embodied in Vedas; Whatever is not free from partiality and unjust, partaking of untruth and like and opposed to the teachings of God embodied in Vedas – that I hold Dharma.

He also said,

> "He who after careful thinking, is ever ready to accept truth and reject falsehood, who counts the happiness of others as he does that of his own self, him I call just."

His message of Vedas was to emphasize respect and regards for other human beings, supported by the Vedic notion of the divine nature of the individual – divine because the body was the temple where the human essence (Soul or Atma) had the possibility to interface with the creator. In the ten principles of Arya Samaj, he enshrined the idea that "All actions should be performed with prime objective of benefiting of mankind" as opposed to dogmatic rituals or revering idols and symbols. The first five principles speak truth and the other five of a society with nobility civics, co-living and disciplined life. In his own life, he interpreted Moksha to be a lower calling (due to its benefit to one individual), than the calling to emancipate other.

Dayananda's 'Back to Vedas' message influenced many thinkers and philosophers the world over.

Dayananda's creation, Arya Samaj, unequivocally condemns idol worship, animal sacrifice, ancestor worship, pilgrimages, priest craft, offerings made in the temples, the caste systems, untouchability, child marriage and discrimination against woman on the grounds that all these lacked Vedic sanction. The Arya Samaj discourages dogma and symbolism and encourages faith in beliefs that runs according to common sense and logic. To many people, Arya Samaj aims to be a 'universal society' based on the authority of Vedas.

However Swami Dayananda showed extreme rationalism and paradoxically made many assumptions while interpreting the Vedas. Thus, he posited that Brahmana could be the only God and denied the existence of lower gods. He also accepted partially the authority of the Shastras, the commentaries of Sayana. It is a matter of surprise that he denied the authority of Shastras, while accepting part of them to be true thus, accepting the Upanayana and disallowing the Shraddha and Ashvameda (the spirits, when summoned according to him were a bad omen and ashva did not mean horse). In order to get around the Shastras he wrote the treatise Sanskaras. Shastras just like the Vedas according to the Sanatana Dharma are correct because of the Yogaja pramana of the Rishis. The god can not either be discovered by senses or by reason.

Some of the princes became his followers. This was a very big blow to those who were, for centuries, carrying on idol worship and irrational religious teachings. This element decided to finish Dayananda. But Dayananda was not deterred by these threats and went on with his mission. In the meanwhile, the strength of his followers increased satisfactorily.

He propounded ten tenets of Arya Samaj which every follower not only know but also follow truly. He also wrote a book *Satyartha Prakasha* (the light of truth), which was widely appreciated by the scholars. The reading of this book was a must for Arya Samajists. By this their minds were enlightened and they took their task of spreading the message of Arya Samaj with more courage and buoyancy. But his opposition, of course did not subside. That element was opposing him on every stage. But he was to carry on, because he had given a word to his Guru to spread the light of Vedas in the minds of the public in general.

So many schools and colleges were established where the teachings of Arya Samaj were taught to the students. Arya Samaj temples were built where the Arya followers sit together and chalk out the future programmes. On the lines of ancient way of imparting the education, Gurukuls were established where the boys and girls (though separately) stayed there the whole time for many years, where they acquire true knowledge and build strong and healthy bodies which can withstand the jerks and pulls throughout the long life. As per the Vedic system, the students who pass from the Gurukuls must follow celibacy up to the age of 25 years. The public in general was very much attracted to the annual functions of these Gurukuls. The people not only donated cash and cereals there but keenly listened to the preaching's of Arya Samaj. By this way, the opposition of Sanatana Dharma blunted and Arya Samaj preachers went freely to the villages for their assigned task.

Once in the year 1883, Nand was the guest to Maharaja Jodhpur, a princely state. He stayed in the rest house and the king was eager to be his follower. One day Dayananda saw the king in the company of a dancer Nanhi Jan. He asked the king to forsake that girl because Aryas do not do such things. She was offended and decided to finish Dayananda.

He was given poison by the cook. He could not survive. But his work is being carried out by Arya Samaj without any hindrance and lethargy. His teachings are being followed not only in India but throughout many countries of the world. The name of Dayananda invokes rational thinking and strong belief in Vedic followings which are free of myths and idol worships. His teachings are as clear as the sunlight at the noon. He is called the harbinger of true knowledge for the humanity as a whole which beacons a healthy mind in a very healthy body.

Because he did not marry therefore he had no offspring. Ten tenets of Arya Samaj founded by Swami Dayananda are:

1. The God is the true source of all knowledge and all materials known through knowledge.
2. God is shapeless, omnipotent, justiceful, kind, omnipresent, immortal therefore only he is worth worshipping.
3. Vedas are the books of all true knowledge. It is the most sacred duty of all Aryans to read, listen and let other read the Vedas.
4. One should be always ready to accept the truth and give up the untruth.

5. All actions should be taken after taking into consideration the truth and untruth.
6. The main work of Arya Samaj is to do good to the whole world – physical, spiritual, and social.
7. All should be treated according to love, social law and ability.
8. Ignorance be banished and knowledge be spread.
9. One should not be pleased with one's progress but the welfare of all should be one's welfare.
10. All people should be obedient to social norms and all should be free to follow the norms for universal welfare.

Martin Luther King, Junior

MARTIN LUTHER KING Junior was born on January 15, 1929 at Atlanta, United States. At the time of birth, his name was Michael King but his father Martin Luther King Senior changed into Martin Luther King. His mother was Alberta Williams King. King was originally sceptical of many Christian claims. Most strikingly was his denial of the bodily resurrection of Jesus during Sunday school at the age of 13. From this point he stated, "doubts began to spring forth unrelentingly. However, he later concluded that Bible has many profound truths which one cannot escape and decided to enter the Seminary. He attended Booker T Washington High School at Atlanta. Being a precocious student, he skipped 9th and 12th grade and entered More House College at the age of 15 without formally doing his high school. In 1948 he graduated from More house with a Bachelor of Arts degree in Sociology and in 1951 he graduated with a Bachelor of Divinity degree. He married Coretta Scot on June 18, 1953.

He became pastor of Dexter Avenue Baptist Church Montgomery, Alabama at age of 25, in 1954. He also received a doctoral degree of philosophy – Systematic Theology. A civil rights leader, theologian and educator Howard Thurman had great influence on him.

Non-Violence

He said, "I am more convinced that the method of non-violent resistances is the most potent weapon available to oppressed people in their struggle for justice and human dignity." African-American civil rights activist Bayard Rustin counselled him to dedicate himself to the principal of non-violence.

Politics

Actually, the Negros have been betrayed by both the Republican and Democratic Party. He therefore maintained a policy of not publicly endorsing a US political party or a candidate. I said, "I do not think the Republican Party is the party full of almighty God nor is the Democratic Party. Both have a weakness towards Negros. Therefore, I am not inextricably bound to either party." He criticised both the parties for their performance on promoting the racial equality. The democrats have betrayed him by capitulating to the whims and caprices of the Southern Dixiecrats. The Republicans have betrayed him by capitulating to the blatant hypocrisy of reactionary right wing northern Republicans. And this coalition of Southern Dixiecrats and right wing reactionary northern republicans defeats every bill and every move towards liberal legislation in the area of civil rights. Although he never publicly, supported a political party or a candidate for president, yet in 1960 he privately voted for John F Kennedy – Kennedy would make the best President on the racial issues. He expressed the view that black Americans as well as other disadvantaged Americans should be compensated for historical wrongs. He once said that granting equality to blacks really does not close the economic gap between them and whites. He continued, he did not seek a full restitution of wages lost to slavery, which is impossible. But he proposed a government compensatory programme of 50 billion dollar over ten years to the disadvantaged groups. He said, "The money spent would be more amply justified by benefits that would accrue to the nation through a spectacular decline in school dropouts, family break ups, crime rates, illegitimacy, swollen, relief rolls, rioting and other social evils." He presented this idea as an application of the common law, regarding settlement of unpaid labour but clarified that he felt that the money should not be spent exclusively on blacks. He stated, it should benefit the disadvantaged of all races. He called for a guaranteed income and was convinced that simple approach will prove to be most effective the solution to poverty is to abolish it directly by a now widely discussed measure the guaranteed income.

Montgomery Bus Boycott, 1955

In March 1955, a fifteen year old girl in Montgomery Claudette Colvin, refused to give up her seat to a white man in compliance with the Jin Crow Laws. King was on the committee which looked in the case, because Colvin was pregnant and unmarried therefore he advocated her case successfully.

Similarly on December 1, 1955 Rosa Park was arrested for refusing the seat. He called for the boycotting the bus service which lasted for 385 days. The situation was so tense that his house was bombed. He was arrested and racial segregation was ended. In 1957 Southern Christian Leadership Conference was founded which was known as SCLC, to harness the moral authority and organizing power of black churches to conduct non-violent protests in the service of civil rights reforms. He led the SCLC until his death. On September 20, 1958 while signing the copy of his book *Stride Toward Freedom* in Blumstein's departmental store, he was stabbed with a letter opener by Izola Curry, a deranged black woman, and he narrowly escaped the death. King applied non-violence to the protests organized by SCLC in 1959. He was suspected to be a communist by Attorney General Robert F Kennedy and FBI was after him, but he continued to work for civil rights for the blacks. King organized and led marches for black right to vote, desegregation labour rights and other basic civil rights. Laws were enacted with the passage of the Civil Rights Act, 1956 and Voting Right Act of 1965.

Albany Movement

It was a desegregation coalition formed in Albany Georgia in November 1961. The movement mobilized thousands of citizens. But King was arrested and sentenced to 45 days jail or a fine of 178 dollars. He chose jail.

Birmingham Campaign

In April 1963, SCLC began a campaign against racial segregation and economic injustice in Birmingham, Alabama. His intent was to provoke mass arrests and create a situation so crisis packed that it will inevitably open the door to negotiation but could not succeed and later on changed the course of campaign by recruiting children and young adults to join the demonstrations. This strategy was called children crusade. High pressure water jets were used by the police against the protesters. The dogs were also let loose on them. Still the protesters were peaceful and campaign was a success. As a result the public places became more open for blacks and his reputation increased immensely. He was arrested, his 13th arrest out of 29 all. He wrote in his cells, "we know through painful experience that freedom is never voluntarily given by oppressors, it must be demanded by the oppressed."

He was a driving force behind intense demonstrations in St Augustine, 1964. The movement was at night through the city and white people attacked them. Hundreds were arrested and jailed.

He and SCLC joined Student Non-Violent Coordinating Committee (SNCC) in Selma, Alabama in December 1964 where SNCC was working on voter registration for several mouths. Due to legal barring the gathering, it halted but King defied the ban and the movement started again.

March on Washington

King represented SCLC during the march to Washington on August 1963 for jobs and freedom. For King the role was quite controversial because he was the key figure who acceded to the wishes of President John F Kennedy in changing the focus of the march. Kennedy initially opposed the march outright because he was concerned it would negatively impact the drive for passage of civil rights legislation. However, the organizers were quite firm that the march would proceed.

He is most famous for his speech 'I Have a Dream' given in front of the Lincoln Memorial during 1963 March on Washington for jobs and freedom. It originally was conceived, as an event to dramatize the desperate condition of the blacks in Southern US and an opportunity to place organizations concern and grievances squarely before the seat of power in nations capital. Organizers Intended to denounce the federal government for its failure to safeguard the civil rights and physical safety of civil right workers and blacks. However, the group acquiesced to presidential pressure and influence and the events ultimately took on a for less strident tone. As a result, some civil right activists felt it presented an inaccurate sanitized pageant of racial harmony. It was called a force on Washington and nation of Islam forbade its members from attending the March.

The march made the specific demands: An end to racial segregation in public schools, meaningful civil right legislation including a law prohibiting racial discrimination in employment, protection of civil right workers from police brutality, a two dollar minimum wage for all workers and self-government for Washington DC then governed by congressional committee. Despite tensions the march was a resounding success.

More than a quarter of a million people of diverse ethnicities attended the event, sprawling the steps of Lincoln Memorial onto the National Hall and around the reflecting pool. At the time, it was the largest gathering of protesters in the history of Washington DC. He delivered a 17 minute speech, later known as 'I Have a Dream'. In the speech the most famous passage – in which he departed from the prepared text, he said: I say to you today my friends, though we face the difficulties of today and tomorrow, I still have a dream. It is a dream deeply rooted in the American dream. I have a dream that one day this nation will rise up and live out the true meaning of its creed: We hold these truths to be self-evident, that all men are created equal. I have a dream that one day on the red hill of Georgia, the sons of former slaves and the sons of former slaves owners will be able to sit down together at the table of brotherhood. I have a dream that one day even the state of Mississippi, a state sweltering with the heat of injustice, sweltering with the heat of oppression, will be transformed into an oasis of freedom and justice. I have a dream that my four little children, will one day live in a nation where they will not be judged by colour of their skin but by the content of their character. I have a dream today, I have a dream that one day, down in Alabama with its vicious racist, with its governor having his lips dripping with words of interposition and nullification one day right there in Alabama, little black boys and girls will able to join hands with little white boys and white girls as sisters and brothers.

'I Have a Dream' came to be regarded as one of the finest speeches in the history of American oratory. This March and specially King's speech, helped put civil rights at the top of the liberal political agenda in the United States and facilitated the passage of the Civil Rights Act of 1964.

Bloody Sunday, 1965

King, James Bevel and SCLC in partial collaboration with SNCC attempted to organize a March from Selma to the state capital of Montgomery on March 7, 1965. The first attempt to march on March 7 was aborted because of the mob and police violence against the demonstrators. This day has since become known as bloody Sunday. It was a major turning point in the efforts to gain public support for the civil Right Movement, the clearest demonstration up to that time of the dramatic potential of King's non-violence strategy.

He met the officials in the Lyndon Johnson Administration on March 5, in order to request an injunction against any prosecution of the demonstrators. He did not attend the march due to church duties but later wrote, "if I had any idea that the state troopers would use the kind of brutality they did, I would have felt compelled to give up my church duties altogether to lead the line of police brutality against protesters, was broadcast extensively and aroused national public outrage." King again attempted a march on March 9. SCLC petitioned for an injunction in federal court against the State of Alabama. This was denied and the judge issued an order blocking the march until after hearing. Nonetheless King led marchers on March 9 to the Edmund Pettus Bridge in Selma, held a short prayer session before turning the marchers around and asking them to disperse so as to not violate the court order. The unexpected ending of this second march aroused the surprise and anger of many within the local movement. The march finally went ahead fully on March 25, 1965. At the conclusion of the march, and on the steps of the state capital, King delivered a speech that became known as 'How Long, Not Long'.

Chicago, 1956

In 1966 after several successes in the South, King and others in civil rights organisations tried to spread the movement to the north with Chicago as their destination. King and Ralph Abernathy both from the middle class, moved into a building at 1550 Hamlin Ave in slums of North Lawdale, Chicago. They demonstrated their support and sympathy for the poor.

The SCLC formed a coalition with CCCO (Coordinating Council of Community Organizations) and started the Chicago Freedom movement. During that spring several white couple/black couple tests of real estate offices uncovered racial steering: Discriminatory processing of housing requests by couples who were exact matches in income, background, number of children and other attributes.

Several larger marches were planned and executed. In Chicago it was quite poor. Even bottles were thrown and screaming throngs, rioting seemed possible. King's beliefs mutilated against his staging a violent event and he negotiated an agreement with Mayor to cancel a march in order to avoid the violence. He received death threats throughout his involvement in the civil rights movement and was hit by a brick during one march but he continued to lead marches in the face of personal danger. The chain stores which did not deal fairly with blacks were targeted under the movement operation Bread basket.

Opposed Vietnam War

King, in 1965 began opposing the Vietnam War because he thought that the money spent there should have been spent for the welfare of the needy people here. This war, he said was not for justice to the poor people but for turning Vietnam, American colony which was not just. He also stated in the speech that true compassion is more than flinging a coin to a beggar. It comes to see that the edifice which produces beggars needs restructuring On January 13, 1968 he took a long march to Washington against the most cruel and senseless war where he declared that they would not support the Government which continued to see the killings of Vietnamese and Americans.

Poor People's Campaign, 1968

In 1968 he and SCLE organized the poor people campaign to address the issues of economic justice. He travelled the country to assemble a multiracial army of poor that would march in Washington to engage in non-violent civil disobedience at the capital until congress created an 'economic bill of rights for poor Americans'. A march was taken to Washington demanding economic aid to the poorest communities of the United States. He opposed spending on war and instead suggested spending on rebuilding the Americans cities so as to cease the hostility to the poors of America. He emphasized reconstruction of the society itself which is the real issue to be faced. He advocated to stop repression on poor people of America and elsewhere. His vision was for change that was more revolutionary than mere reforms.

Assassination and Aftermath

On March 29, 1968 King went to Memphis, in support of black sanitary public works employees who had been on strike since March 12 for higher wages and better treatment. In one incident, black street repairman received pay for two hours when they were sent home because of bad weather but whites were paid for full day.

On April 3, he addressed a rally and delivered his 'I Have Been to the Mountaintop' address at Mason Temple. King's flight to Memphis had been delayed by a bomb threat against his plane. At the close of his last speech of his career in reference to the bomb threat he said:

> "And some began to say the threats or talk about threats that were out. What would happen to me from some of our sick white brothers? Well I do not know what will happen now. We have got some difficult days ahead. But it does not matter with me now, because I have been to the mountaintop. And I do not mind. Like anybody, I would like to live a long life. Longevity has its place. But I am not concerned about that now. I just want to do God's will. And he has allowed me to go up to the mountain. I have looked over and I have seen the promised land. I may not get there with you. But I want you to know tonight, that we as a people, will get to the promised land so I am happy to night. I am not worried about any thing. I am not fearing any man. Mine eyes have seen the glory of the coming of the lord."

He was in a hotel at Memphis. One Abernathy was already there who testified to the US House select committee on his assassination. King talked to the musician in the balcony. These were his last words. He said to the musician Ben Branch: "Ben make sure you play 'Take My Hand, Precious Lord', in the meeting tonight play it really pretty."

On 4 April 1968 at 6 PM a shot range out as King stood on the balcony. The bullet entered through his right check, smashing his jaw, Then went down his spinal cord before lodging in his shoulder. After an emergency surgery of the chest he was pronounced dead. They say that at 39 his heart was 60 years old.

It led to nationwide riots. President Lyndon B Johnson declared national mourning for this civil right leader. Even Vice-President Hurbert Humphrey attended his funeral on behalf of the President. It was said, "he tried to feed the hungry, clothe the naked and be right on the war question, he with a love served the humanity." His killer was caught after two months. He was James Earl Ray. He was sentenced to a 99 year prison term. Although there were allegations of his being communist but King always denied. But after his speech 'I Have a Dream', FBI described him the most dangerous and effective leader of the Negros, in the country. King said, "The Negro revolution is a genuine revolution born from the same worm that brought all social massive upheavals intolerable conditions and unendurable situations."

King Martin Luther Junior was born to a revolutionary and he carried out the unfinished task of his father. As the father fought for the genuine rights, for the negros, the son was fully determined to bring negros on equal pedestal of the whites. The Negros were the real inhabitants of America and still they were under the subjugation of those who came from outside from far off. This fact always pinched the father and the son took the flag till his death. Those who work for the betterment of the others even at the risk of the life are the great person. Therefore, he was the great person without any ifs and buts. He was killed at the age of 39. Had he lived longer he would have carried the flame burning likewise unmindful of sufferings and hateful propaganda against him of his being communist. A religious person from the origin King fought like the best warrior and never retrieved and repented of his doings in the life. But otherwise he gained courage and strength from the successful steps he took fully determined, for the rights of the rightful people. It was due to his far-reaching greatness that now Obama is ruling the super power of the world. We wish he would have lived a long life for the sake of the humanity.

Nelson Mandela

NELSON MANDELA was born on 18th July 1918 in a very small village Mvezo in Eastern Cape province of South Africa. His father was Gadla Henry who was the chief of the town. When he was nine his father expired. In the family, he was the first to go to school. When he was sixteen he joined a boarding institute. When he was 19 he took interest in boxing. He completed his junior certificate in two years instead of the usual three years. After that he moved to college in Fort Beaufort. At Fort Hare university where he was for a BA course, he met Oliver Tambo, his life-long friend. Initially he found an employment as a Guard at a mine. But his service was soon terminated. He started work as an article clerk for a Johannesburg law firm. He completed his BA there via correspondence. He joined law studies where he was with Joo Salo who eventfully became minister in his cabinet.

After his 1948 election victory of the Afrikaner dominated National Party which supported the apartheid policy of racial segregation, he joined politics. He lead prominently in the ANCS 1952 Defiance campaign and the 1955 congress of people whose adoption of the freedom charter provided the fundamental basis of an anti-apartheid cause. During this time, he and a fellow lawyer Oliver Tambo operated the law firm providing free law to many blacks. He took part in anti-apartheid activities. Along with 150 others he was arrested on December 5, 1956 and was charged with treason. The Marathon Treason Trial of 1956-61 followed and he got acquittal.

From 1952-59, a new class of black activities known as the Africanists disrupted ANC activities in the townships demanding more drastic steps against the National party regime. The ANC leadership under Tambo and Sisula felt not only that Africanists were moving too fast but also that they challenged their leadership. The ANC leadership consequently bolstered their position through alliances with small White coloured and Indian political parties in an attempt to give appearance of a wider appeal than Africanists. The Africanists ridiculed the 1955 freedom charter for concession of 1,00,000 strong ANC to just a single vote in congressional alliance. Four Secretary Generals of the five participating parties secretly belonged to reconstituted South African Communist Party (SACP). In 1959 ANC lost its most militant support when most of the Africanists, with financial support from Ghana and political support from Transval based Basotho broke away to form Pan-Africanist Congress (PAC) under the direction of Sobukwe and Leball.

Armed Anti-Apartheid Activities

In 1961 he became leader of ANC's armed wing. He coordinated sabotage campaigns wing. He coordinated sabotage campaigns against military and Government targets, making plans for possible guerrilla war if sabotage failed to end apartheid. He raised funds and arranged paramilitary training of the group.

A fellow ANC member, Kodesh, explains the bombing campaign led by Mandela "When we knew that we are going to start on 16 December 1961 to blast the symbolic places of apartheid like pass offices, courts, post offices in such a way that no one to be killed."

Mandela described the move to armed struggle as a last resort, years of increasing repression and violence from the state convinced him that many years of non-violent protest against apartheid had not and could not achieve any progress. In June 1961, he sent a letter to South African newspapers warning the government that if they did not meet the demands, we shall embark on a campaign of sabotage. The letter demanded the Government to accept a call for National Constitutional Convention. The demand were not met by the government and beginning on 16 December 1961, the Umkhonto we Sizwe (his organization) with Mandela as its leader launched a bombing campaign against Government targets with first action of the campaign being the electricity station. In total over the next 18 months we shall initiate more dozen acts of sabotages and bombing. The South African Government alleged more acts of sabotage had been carried out and at the Rivonia trial the accused would be charged with 193 acts of sabotage in total. The campaign of sabotage against the Government included attacks on posts, machines, power facilities and even crop burning at various places including Johannesburg, port Elizabeth and Durban.

Later in 1980, MK, the organisation co-founded by him, waged a guerrilla war against apartheid Government in which many civilians became casualties. At Church street 19 people were killed. He admitted that MK violated human rights also. He was a declared terrorist and until July 2008 he was barred from entering United States without a waiver from the US secretary of states.

His Arrest and Rivonia Trial

On 5 August 1962 he was arrested after living on the run for 17 months and was imprisoned in the Johannesburg Fort. He attributed this arrest to his own carelessness in concealing his whereabouts. He was linked to CIA also. After three days, charges of leading the workers to strike in 1961, leaving the country illegally he was awarded five years jail.

While Mandela was in prison, police arrested ANC leaders on 11 July 1963. He was brought there and at Rivonia trial they were charged for four charges of the capital crimes of sabotages, which he admitted, these crimes were equivalent to treason. The charge sheet listed 193 acts of sabotage. They were charged with the preparation, manufacture of explosives, including 2,10,000 hand grenades, 48,000 anti-personnel mines, 1,500 time devices, 144 tonnes of Ammonium Nitrate, 21.6 tonnes of Aluminium powder and a tonne of black powder. The plot of foreign invasion of South Africa was also the charge – which he denied. Other charges were admitted by him.

He on April 20, 1964 laid out reasoning at Pretoria Supreme Court, choice to use violence as a tactic. He also described how his party had used peaceful means to resist apartheid for years until the Sharpeville Massacre. That event coupled with the referendum establishing the Republic of South Africa and declaration of the state of emergency along with banning the ANC made it clear to him that sabotage was the only choice. Otherwise it would tantamount to surrender. He went on to explain how they developed the manifesto of Umkhonto we Sizwe on 16 December 1961 intent an exposing the failure of National party's policies after economy would be threatened by foreigners unwillingness to risk investing in the country. He closed with these words, "During my life time I have dedicated myself to the struggle of the African people. I have fought against white domination, and I have fought against black domination. I have cherished the ideal of a democratic and free society in which all persons live together in harmony and with equal opportunities. It is an ideal which I hope to live for and to achieve. But if need be, it is an ideal for which I am fully prepared to die."

They were found guilty and were sentenced to life imprisonment on June 1964. The Amnesty people campaigned against the harsh conditions Mandela experienced while in prison.

He was kept on Robben Island for 18 months of his 27 years in prison. In jail his reputation grew and he became widely known as the most significant Black Leader of South Africa. He and others were put to work in the lime quarry. The prisoners were segregated by race with the blacks getting fewest rations. He was a 'D' class prisoner – the lowest class with fewest privileges. Only one visitor and one letter in six months. The letters were defaced rendering them unreadable.

When he was in prison, Mandela took study with University of London by correspondence through its external programme and received the degree of laws. He was subsequently nominated for the position of Chancellor of University of London in the 1981 election but lost to Princess Anne.

There was also a plot to rescue him out of prison in 1969. But the plot was infiltrated by Winter on behalf of South African intelligence. Actually the plot was foiled by Britain Secret Intelligence Service.

He was transferred to Pollismoor prison. This move was to remove the influence of this person on young black activists in Robben Island prison, which was nicknamed – Mandela University.

In February 1985 President PW Botha offered Mandela his freedom on condition that he unconditionally rejected violence as a political weapon despite the advice of his cabinet. This was because they knew that Mandela would never commit his organisation to give up the armed struggle in exchange for personal freedom. He indeed spurned the offer saying, "what freedom am I being offered while the organisation of the people remains banned? Only free men can negotiate. A prisoner cannot enter the contracts."

However, no progress was made and he was moved to Victor Vorster prison and remained there till his release. Restrictions, some of them were removed. Throughout his imprisonment local and international pressure mounted on South African Government to release him under the resounding slogans – free Nelson Mandela. In 1989 South Africa reached a cross road when Botha suffered a stroke and was replaced by Frederik Willem de Klerk. De Klerk announced his release in February 1990.

He was visited several times by delegates of the international committee of Red Cross while at Robben Island and later at Pollsmoor prison. He had this to say about the visits, "to me personally and those who shared the experience of being political prisoners, the red cross was a beacon of humanity within the dark inhumane world of political prison imprisonment."

Release

On February 2, 1990 President De Klerk reversed the ban on ANC and other anti-apartheid organisations and announced that Mandela would shortly be released from prison. Mandela was released from Victor Vorster prison on 11 February 1990. This even was broadcast live all over the world.

On the day of his release he made a speech to the nation. He declared his commitment to peace and reconciliation with country's white minority but made it clear that ANC's armed struggle was not yet over when he said, "our resort to armed struggle in 1960 with formation of military wing of ANC was a purely defensive action against the violence of apartheid. The factors which necessitated still exist today. We have no option but to continue. We express the hope that a climate conducive to a negotiated settlement would be created soon so that there may no longer be the need of armed struggle." He also said, his main focus was to bring peace to the black majority.

Negotiations

Following his release from prison he returned to the ANC leadership. From 1990 to 1994 he led the party in the multiparty negotiations that led country multiracial election.

In 1991 ANC held its first national conference after its unbanning, electing him as President of the organisation. His old friend and colleague Oliver Tambo who had lead the organisation in exile during Mandela's imprisonment became National Chairperson.

His leadership through the negotiations as well as his relationship with President De Klerk was recognized when they were jointly awarded Nobel Peace Prize in 1993. However, the relationship was sometimes strained, particularly so in a sharp exchange in 1991 when he furiously referred to De Klerk as the head of an illegitimate, discredited minority regime. Talks broke down following the Boipatong massacre in June 1992 when he took ANC out of negotiations assuming De Klerk's complicity in the killings. However, talks resumed following the Bisho massacre in September 1992. When the spectre of violent confrontation made it clear that the negotiations were the only way forward.

Following the assassination of ANC leader Chris Hani in April 1993, there were renewed fears that the country would erupt in violence. He addressed the nation appealing for calm, in a speech regarded as Presidential even though he was not yet so. He said, "tonight I am reaching out to every single South African, Black and White, from the very depth of my being. A white man full of prejudice and hate came to our country and committed a deed so foul that our nation now teeters on the brink of disaster. A white woman of Afrikaner origin, risked her life so that we may know and bring to justice this assassin. This is the time to stand united against those who want to destroy the peace."

'Kill the Boers' Controversy

Following the 7 September 1992 Bhiso massacre, on September 8, at the memorial service for the 28 massacred protesters, Nelson Mandela and the freedom fighters are recorded video singing a song in Xhosa whose lyrics include, "Go safely we the members of MK have pledged ourselves to kill the Boers." The video footage caused controversy in July 2007 when Right wing Group with links to Bocremag, another ring wing group with white separatist aims spread DVDs containing the footage to various people across the country.

Presidency of the Country

South Africa's first multiracial elections in which full enfranchisement was granted, were held on 27 April 1994. The ANC won 62% of the votes in the election and Mandela as a leader of ANC, was inaugurated on May 10, 1994, as country's first black President with National Party's De Klerk as his first deputy and Thabo Mbeki as second in the Government of National Unity. As President from May 1994 to June 1999 Mandela presided over the transition from minority rule and apartheid winning, international respect for his advocacy of National and International reconciliation. He encouraged Black South Africans to get behind the previously hated Springboks as South Africa hosted the 1995 Rugby World Cup. He handed over the cup to the winning team of his country which was all white. By this he won the world's praise.

After assuming the presidency, one of Mandela trademarks was his use of Batik shirt, known as Madiba shirt, even on formal occasions. In South Africa's first post apartheid military operation Mandela ordered troops into Lesotho in September 1998 to protect the Government of Prime Minister Pakalitha Mosisili. This came after a disputed election prompt fierce opposition threatening the unstable Government.

During his presidency, a wide range of progressive social reforms were enacted by his Government, aimed at reducing long entrenched social and economic inequalities in South Africa, free health care for all children under the age of six was introduced in 1994, together with pregnant and breast feeding women making use of public sector health facilities free. Reconstruction and development programmes were launched, which invested in essential social services such as housing and health care. Increase in welfare spending were carried out with public spending on welfare and social grants to substantial extent. The government also introduced the parity in grants for communities including disability grants, child maintenance grants, and old age pensions, which had previously been set at different levels for South Africans different racial groups. Child maintenance grant was extended to blacks in rural areas who were previously excluded from the system, public spending in education was increased.

The Land Restitution Act of 1994 enabled people who had lost their property as a result of Natives Land Act, 1913 to claim back their land, leading to settlement of tens of thousands of land claims. The Land Reform Act 3 of 1996 safe guarded the rights of labour tenants and live and grow crops and graze live stocks on farms. This legislation ensured that such tenants could not be evicted without a court order or if they were over the age of 65. Child support grants were introduced in 1998 to alleviate child poverty. While the Skill Development Act of 1998 provided for the establishment of mechanisms to finance and promote skills development at the workplace.

Labour Relation Act of 1995 which promoted workplace democracy, orderly collective bargaining and effective resolution of labour disputes. Basic Condition Employment Act of 1997 improved enforcement mechanism while extending an impressed 'floor' of rights to all workers, while the Employment Equity Act of 1998 was passed to end unfair discrimination and ensure the implementation of affirmative action in the work place.

Compulsory schooling was introduced for African children between six and fourteen years while free meals were provided for school children.

Amendments to Aged Persons Act in 1998 which provided for the homes for elderly and prevent the abuse of elderly persons. The prevention of illegal eviction from and unlawful Occupation of Land Act of 1998 provided that no individual may by evicted from his home without a court order after all relevant circumstances have been taken into account.

National Development Agency was established in 1998, was mandated to provide funds to civil society organisations, to meet the development needs of the poor people. The extension of Security Tenure Act of 1997 aimed at providing security tenure to vulnerable occupants of land out of the urban area. This contained provisions which sought to create and support long-term security for vulnerable occupants while also safe guarding them from an unfair eviction.

And thus, many other acts for the safety of the public in general were passed to save them from unfair harassment by the government agencies and the moneylenders.

Lockerbie Trial

President Mandela took particular interest in helping to resolve, the long running dispute between Gaddafi's Libya on one hand and England on the other, over bringing to trial the two Libyans who were indicted in November 1991 and accused of sabotaging Pan AM flight which crashed at the Scottish town of Lockerbie on 21 December 1988, with the loss of 270 lives. His famous declaration was the sole means of solution: "No one should be complainant, prosecutor and Judge."

When Mandela was a student, South Africa, his country was under the rule of the white minority, where 90% original inhabitants were under 10% white people who came from far off. He decided to liberate his people. He suffered immensely and suffering long time imprisonment for the sake of his people. Ultimately, he succeeded in his determination and became the President. At this also, he reconciled with those who were using very hard methods to keep the black under their thumb. He was awarded the Nobel Peace Prize for his remarkable achievement. He managed to pass laws to bring the suppressed people at par with those who were harassing them for the last so many years. He took presidency only for one term and passed it to his long time colleague and deputy on 14 June 1999 and is guiding him from outside. He got the respect of his people and that of white minority. Therefore, he is a great man of the world. It is usually seen that if one once gets the power then he goes on clinging over till removed with disgrace. But Mandela left honourably and is still a respectable and loving leader of his people – really a great achievement.

Alexander the Great

ALEXANDER was born on 20 July 356 BC in Pella the capital of ancient Greek kingdom of Macedon. He was the son of king Macedon Philip–II and his fourth wife Olympians, the daughter of Neoptolemus king of Epirus. On the day Alexander was born, his father was preparing a siege on the city of Botidea. The same day he received an information that his general has won a battle and his horses have won a race at the Olympic games. It all showed that Alexander was destined for greatness. He was raised by a nurse Lanika, sister of Cleitus, his future general and tutored by the strict Leonedas, a relative of his mother. He was raised in the manner of a noble Macedonian youth learning to read, play, lyre, ride, fight and hunt.

When he was ten years old, some trader brought a horse to be sold to his father. The horse refused to be mounted. Alexander who detected the horses fear of its own shadow asked to tame it and eventually he did. Philips overjoyed at this display of courage and ambition, kissed his son tearfully and said, "My son, you must find a kingdom large enough for your ambitions, Macedon is too small for you." He bought the horse for him. Alexander named it Buecphlas, meaning 'ox-head'. This horse carried Alexander up to Pakistan. When the animal died of old age, he named a city after him.

When he was 13 his father chose Aristotle hit tutor and he agreed only when his father agreed to rebuild Aristotle's home town Stageria which Philip raised some time back. At the age of 16 Alexander's education under Aristotle ended. His father went for a war against Byzantion leaving him incharge of the kingdom. He responded quickly against a revolt. Upon Philip return he was dispatched with a force to subdue revolts in southern Thrace. Campaigning against the Greek city of Perinthus, Alexander saved the life of his father. He was also sent for a campaign in Greek. He also repulsed a attack by rebels. He was with his father when Philip was raising the battle of Chaeronea. There was a bitter fight. Philips ordered his troops to press forward and on the other side Alexander attacked the enemy with full force and compelled the enemy to surrender.

His father married Cleopatra much younger in age. Her uncle wanted that Philip's heir should be the son of his niece. At this Alexander shouted, "You villain, what, am I then a bastard?" He fled Macedon with his mother to his maternal uncle, king of Epirus in Modona. He left his mother there and went to Illyrian king and sought refuse. He was treated as a welcome guest despite having defeated them in a battle few years back. But his father never wanted to disown such a brave son. He sent a family friend who brought Alexander back.

In 336 BC Philip was assassinated by his body guards. Alexander was proclaimed king of Macedon by the nobles and the army at the age of 20. He began his reign by eliminating the potential rivals to the throne. News of Philips death raised many states in revolt, including Thebes, Athens, Thessaly and tribes of northern Macedon. He responded very quickly and subdued them with a strong hand. The famous encounter between Alexander and Diogenes the cynic occurred during his stay in Corinth. When he asked Diogenes what he could do for him, the philosopher disdainfully asked him to stand a little to the side as he was blocking the sunlight. The reply apparently delighted Alexander, who is said to have said, "But verily, I were not Alexander, I would like to be Diogenes." At Corinth, Alexander took the title of 'Hegemony' (leader).

Before crossing to Asia Alexander wanted to safeguard his northern boarders. In spring 335 BC, he advanced to suppress several revolts. Starting from Amphibolies, he travelled east into the country of the Traecans and at mount Hermus, his army attacked and defeated the Treacan forces manning heights. He also marched to Tribali and defeated their army.

Alexander then marched for three days to Danube encountering the tribes there on the opposite shore crossing the river at night. He surprised them and forced their army to retreat. Then news reached him that Cleitus, king of Illyria and king Glankias were in open revolt. Alexander defeated them and forced them to flee. Thus, he made secure his northern frontier.

He then set out for Asian campaign leaving Antipater as regent. His army crossed the Hellespont in 334 BC with 48,000 soldiers, 6,000 cavalry and a fleet of 120 ships with crews numbering 38,000. He showed his intent to conquer the entirety of Persian empire by throwing a spear into the Asian social and saying, he accepted Asian as a gift from the gods. This also showed Alexander's eagerness to fight in contrast to his father's preference for diplomacy.

After an initial victory against Persian forces at the Battle of Granicus, Alexander accepted the surrender of the Persian provincial capital and treasury of Sardis and proceeded along the Ionian Coast. He left the Government of Caria to Ada who adopted Alexander. From there, he proceeded to Lycia asserting control over all coastal cities to deny the Persian naval bases. There was no major port. At the ancient Phrygian capital Gordian Alexander 'undid' the hither to unsolved Gordean Knot, a feat said to await the future king of Asia.

According to the story, Alexander proclaimed that it did not matter how the knot was undone and hacked it apart with his sword.

After spending the winter campaigning in Asia Minor, his army crossed the Ciliecan gates in 333 BC, and defeated the main Persian army under the command Darius. Darius fled the battle causing his army to collapse and left behind his wife, his two daughters, his mother and a fabulous treasure. He offered peace treaty that included the land already lost and ransom of 10,000 talents for his family. Alexander replied that since he was now king of Asia it was he alone who decided the territorial divisions.

Alexander proceeded to take possession of Syria and most of the cost of the Levant. In the following year he was forced to attack Tyre which he captured after a long and difficult siege. He got all the men of military age massacred and sold the women and children into slavery.

When he destroyed Tyre most of the towns on the route to Egypt quickly capitulated with the exception of Gaza. The strong hold at Gaza was heavily fortified and built on a hill requiring a siege. After three unsuccessful attempts the strong hold fell but not before he had received a serious shoulder wound. As in Tyre, all the men of military age were put to the sword and the women and children were sold into slavery. Jerusalem instead opened its gates in surrender and he was shown the Book of Daniels prophecy, presumably Chapter 8 which described a mighty Greek King who would conquer the Persian Empire. He spared Jerusalem and pushed into Egypt.

In later 332 BC he advanced on Egypt where he was regarded as liberator. He was called 'new master of universe' and son of deity of Amun. Hence forth he was referred to Zeus – Amman as his true father and currency depicted him adorned with rams horn as a symbol of his divinity. During his stay in Egypt he founded Alexandria-by-Egypt which would become the prosperous capital of Ptolemaic kingdom after his death.

He left Egypt in 331 BC and marched eastward into Mesopotamia (now northern Iraq) and again defeated Darius. Darius again left the field and fled and Alexander chased him as far as Arbela. Gaugamela was for the final encounter for the two and Alexander captured Babylon.

From Babylon he went to Susa, one of the Achaemenid capitals and captured the legendary treasury. He sent the bulk of his army to the Persian ceremonial capital of Persepolis via the Royal Road. He himself took the selected troops on direct route to the city. He was to storm the pass of the Persian gates which had been blocked by Persian army under Arwbarzanes and then hurried to Persepolis before its garrison could loot the treasury.

He then chased Darius, first into Media and then to Parthia. The Persian king no longer controlled his own destiny and was taken prisoner his kins. The kins killed him. Bessus became his successor.

Bessus launched a guerrilla campaign against Alexander. Alexander set out to punish Bessus. This campaign became the grand tour of Central Asia. He founded new cities, all called Alexandria including modern Kandhar in Afghanistan.

During this time he took the title 'King of Kings' (Shahanshah) and adopted elements of Persian dress and customs – notably a symbolic kissing of the hand or prostration on the ground which Persians showed to their suspensors. The Greeks regarded the gesture as the province of deities and believed that Alexander meant to deify himself by requiring it. This cost him the sympathies of many of his countrymen and eventually he abandoned it.

A plot against his life was revealed and one of his officers Philters was executed for failing to alert Alexander. The death of the son necessitated the death of the father and thus Parmenion who had been charged with guarding the treasury at Ecbatana was also assassinated to prevent the attempt of vengeance. Most infamously, he killed the man who saved his life at Granieus, during a violent drunken altercation at Maracanda (Samarkand) in which Clicits accused Alexander of several judgements of mistakes and most especially, having forgot the Macedonian ways in favour of corrupt oriental life styles.

Later in the Central Asian campaign a second plot against his life was revealed, this one was instigated by his own royal 'Pages'. His official historian Callisthenes was implicated in the plot, however historian are yet to confirm.

When he set out for Asia, he left general Antipater, an experienced military and political leader incharge of his kingdom, Macedon. His sacking of Thebes ensured that Greece remained quiet in his absence. One exception was a call to arms by Spartan King Agisin in 331 BC. Antipater referred the Spartans punishments to Alexander who chose to pardon them. There was also considerable friction between Antipater and Olympians and they complained to Alexander about each other.

In general, Greece enjoyed a period of peace and prosperity during Alexander's absence. He sent back vast sum of money from his conquests which stimulated the economy and increased the trade across the empire. However his constant demand for troops and migration of Macedonians throughout his empire depleted manpower there, greatly weakening it in the years after him and ultimately led to subjugation by Rome. No doubt his eye was constantly over his kingdom where so ever he had been.

After the death of Spitamenes and his marriage to Roxana to cement relations with his new satrapies Alexander turned to the Indian Subcontinent. He invited the chieftains of former satrapy of Gandhara in north of what is now Pakistan to come to him and submit to his authority. Omphics ruler of Taxila whose kingdom extended from the Indus to the Hydaspes, complied, but the chieftains of some hill clans including the Aspasia and Assakano sections of the Kambojas refused to summit. In the winter of 327/326 BC Alexander personally led a campaign against these clans – Kumar, Sneat and Bunir valleys. A very fierce contest ensued in which Alexander was wounded in the shoulder by a dart but eventually they lost. Alexander then faced Assakenoil who fought in the strong hold of Massage, Orn and Aronos. The fort of Massage reduced only after days of bloody fighting in which he was wounded seriously in the ankle. He not only slaughtered the entire population of Massage but also reduced the houses to rubles. A similar slaughter followed at Ora. At this several people fled to the fortress of Aornos and he followed close behind and captured the strong fort on the hill after four days fight. He then crossed Indus and fought the epic battle with king Porus who ruled a region of Punjab then, in 326 BC. Alexander though defeated Porus yet was greatly impressed by the bravery of Porus. When Porus brought to him, he asked what should be done to him. At this Porus replied, what a winning king should do with the defeated one.

At this Alexander was greatly impressed and made him his ally and appointed Porus as his satrap and also added some territory in Porus kingdom which earlier was not there. Choosing a local helped him to control these distant territories. It is told that Alexander's loving horse died here and he founded a city in its name Bucephale He also founded another city Nicacea means victory, located at the site of modern Mong, Punjab.

East of Pours kingdom, near the Ganga river were the Nand empire of Magadha and further east the Gangridai expire of Bengal. Fearing the prospect of facing other large armies and exhausted by years of campaigning Alexander's army mutinied at Hyphenise river, refusing to march further east. This river thus marks the easternmost extent of his conquests.

As for the Macedonians however, their struggle with Porus blunted their courage and stayed their further advance into India. For having had all they could do to repulse an enemy who mustered only twenty thousand infantry and two thousand horses, they very violently opposed Alexander when he insisted on crossing the river Ganga also, width of which, as they learned was thirty two furling, its depth a hundred fathoms, while its banks on the further side were covered with multitudes of men at arms and horse men and elephants.

For, they were told that the kings of Ganderites and Parasail were awaiting them with eighty thousand horse men, two hundred thousand footmen, eighty thousand chariots and six thousands war elephants. He tried to persuade his soldiers to march further, but his general Coenus pleaded to change his opinion and return. He said their wives and children are longing to see them for a long period. He at last agreed and turned south marching along Indus. Along the way his army conquered the Mali clans modern day Multan and other Indian tribes.

He sent much of his army to Carmine – modern Iran, with General Crateus and commissioned a fleet to explore the Persian Gulf shore, while he led the rest back to Persia through more difficult route along Gedrosian desert and Makran. He reached Susa in 324 BC but not before losing many men to the harsh desert.

Last Years in Persia

Discovering that many of his satraps and military governors had misbehaved in his absence, Alexander executed several of them. As a gesture of thanks he paid off the debits of his soldiers and announced, that he would send over aged and disabled veterans back to Macedon, led by Craterous. His troops misunderstood his intention and mutinied at the town of Opis. They refused to be sent away.

After three days, unable to persuade his men back down, Alexander gave Persians command posts in army and conferred military titles upon Persian units. They quickly begged pardon which he accepted and had a great banquet for several thousands of his men in which he ate with them. In an attempt to craft lasting harmony between his Macedonian and Persian subjects, he held a man marriage of his senior officers with Persian and other noble women at Susa. Meanwhile, upon his return he learned that guards of the tomb of the Cyrus the Great had desecrated it, and he swiftly executed them.

Afterwards he travelled to Ecbatana to retrieve the bulk of the Persian treasure when his close friend, Hephaestus died of illness. This death devastated him and he ordered the preparation of an expensive funeral pyre in Babylon, as well as a decree for public mourning.

Death and Succession

On June 10,323 BC he died in the palace in Babylon at the age 32. They say that he spent a night and next day drinking with Medius of Larissa, he developed fever which worsened his health and he was unable to speak. The soldiers were allowed to file past him as he silently waved at them. He thereafter died of agony.

After the death of Alexander his general Salukus became the king of the Eastern part of his kingdom. He wanted to expand his kingdom towards India. Therefore, he invaded western India in 305 BC. But he was defeated by king Chandragupta. As a result, he signed a peace treaty and even married his daughter Helind to Chandragupta. He also gave in gift the area up to Hindu Kush and appointed his ambassador, Magasthenes at the capital of Chandragupta. Salukas got 500 elephants in return gift from Chandragupta.

This invasion of Alexander on India became very conducive for communication between Unan and India. The traders and the craft men of Unan came to India in large number and vice versa. This resulted in better supplies and improvement of the skill on both sides. This also influenced the cultural exchanges and the science of astrology.

Alexander had leadership quality since very youth. He was full of self-confidence. He was fully taught the lessons of bravery and steadfastness. Just to buttress his self-confidence he was always praised for his small successes. This enabled him to cross the barriers of traditional influence and area of operation for a king of his status. His success even during challenging circumstance paved his way to other successes during grim situations. His Guru Aristotle always taught him not to look backward but only forward which was the word in his dictionary. But the success against king Porus of India prompted him to retrace simply because of the unfavourable circumstances for his troops which were afraid for their health and prevailing living conditions. Otherwise he himself was never satisfied with his victories. He was to achieve countless victories so that his name could be on the top of warriors.

Alexander did not know hesitation because he was taught to do any work with full preparation and confidence. The world victory required full preparedness and deep thinking. Because the half-heartedness is enemy to the success therefore he was taught the abundance confidence and was made the volcano of strength. Otherwise how could he think of world victory? The full preparedness never let the person to falter. Therefore, he was beyond ifs and buts but full of mind and heart of winning any war what so ever of any magnitude and vicissitude may it be. He must have been taught not to be inferior but far far superior of the kings and king of kings. The teaching of his Guru Aristotle made him hard, bodily and heartily.

But, when he was dying he was in a mood of repentance. He uttered that what for he killed Dara. Dara also was a very brave king. He was killed at his hands after he was defeated in the war. The killing of the brave man was a loss to the humanity as a whole. Therefore, Alexander was not great himself but he had full respect for the other brave persons. He did not kill Porus and instead returned his kingdom. He was a very great man really.

Adolf Hitler

ADOLF HITLER was born in Braunau am Inn, a little town situated just on the frontier of Germany and Austria. His father Alois was a civil servant and mother Klara was a housewife. His father was in Austrian service. At the age of 56, his father retired and settled at Lam Bach in upper Austria as a farmer. It was there that Hitler began to have ideals of his own. He used to mix with the roughest boys which caused his mother many anxious moments. He did not want to follow the career of his father. His speaking power began to develop and he used to have strenuous arguments with his comrades. He became a juvenile ring leader who was difficult to manage at school. In his free time, he practised singing in the choir of the monastery church at Lam Bach, His father thought that he would be priest at a village church. But his oratorical gift did not suit his father. When he was eleven years old he started opposing any idea to which he set little or no value. He also refused to be a civil servant. Then his father suggested to him to be an artist painter. But he refused.

At that time Austria was a multinational state. Germans were a part of it. This was the major point for his future. When he was 13 years old his father died. His mother wished that he should continue his studies as per the wish of his father. Two years later his mother also died. Poverty and the stern reality forced him to decide what to do.

He packed his clothes and with a indomitable resolution in his heart he left for Vienna. He was determined to become something.

He sat for the entrance examination for the Academy of Fine Arts. He was fully hopeful about the coming success. But the result was quite otherwise. He failed. Therefore he could not become an architect. This incident made him quite tough. He, then within thanked the failure because he was thrown into the world of misery and poverty and thus, he came to know the people for whom he was, afterwards to fight. His eyes opened to two perils the name of which he scarcely knew hither to and had no notion what so ever of their terrible significance for the existence of German people. These two perils were Marxism and Judaism for the common people living in Vienna means happy living but for him it was the sadist period of his life. Even after many years, the mention of Vienna aroused within him the gloomy thoughts. He even denied himself food for days together. The books were his only help during that period after days of manual labour.

After two years there, he gained a clear understanding of Social Democracy, in its teachings and technique of its operation. He recognized the infamy of that technique whereby the movement carried on a campaign of mental terrorism against bourgeoisie who were neither morally nor spiritually equipped to withstand the attacks. The tactics of Social Democracy consisted in opening at given signal, a veritable drum-fie of all lies and calumnies against the man whom they believed to be the most redoubtable of their adversaries, until the nerves, the latter gave way and they sacrificed the man who was attacked simply in the hope being allowed to live in peace. But the hope proved always to be foolish one, for they were never left in peace. The same tactics are repeated again and again until fear of these mad dogs exercises, through suggestion, a paralyzing effect on their victim. The Social Democrats know how to create the impression that they alone are the protectors of peace. They used the quiet intimidation and at another time by sheer day light robbery. He also came to understand that physical intimidation has its significance for the man as well as individual. Here, again the Socialists had to calculate accurately the psychological effect.

The impression which such successful tactics make on the minds of the broad masses, whether they be adherents or opponents, can be estimated only by one who knows the popular mind not from books but from practical life. The more he understood the method of physical intimidation the more sympathy he had for the multitude that had succumbed to it. There were millions and millions of workmen who began by being hostile to the Social Democratic Party but their defences were repeatedly stormed and finally they had to surrender. Yet this defeat was due to stupidity of bourgeois parties who had opposed every social demand put forwarded by the working classes. They posed as if they alone stand for working classes.

Hitler had been observing the excesses of the Jews upon the general masses. Those who protested were brutally put to end. He saw excesses through press, excesses through publicity and excesses through art, excesses through literature and excesses through Theatre. He also saw the part Jews played in social phenomenon of prostitution and in white slave traffic. A cold shiver ran down his spine when he first ascertained that it was the same cold blooded, thick skinned and shameless Jew who showed his consummate skill in conducting that revolting exploitation of the dregs of city. Then he became fired with wrath. He decided to bring to light this problem in all its details. One could care such a malady temporarily but only for some days or at least for a year. But, on his meeting those who believed to have been converted he found that they had become as they were before. That malady against, Nature held them once again in its clutches. Gradually he became an expert in the doctrine of the Marxists and he used this knowledge as an instrument to drive home his own firm conviction.

After learning the very hard lesson of life in Vienna he moved to Munich in 1912. During the period he lived at Vienna he used to look upon Germany as an imperturbable colossus. But here his opinion changed. The spiritual and moral decline of German people had set in, though those who were affected by the morbid decadence were frequently unaware of the forces which were breaking up their existence. But since nobody recognized or wanted to recognize the real cause of disease that way of combating Marxism was no more effective.

As a boy or as a young man he longed for the occasion to prove that his national enthusiasm was not mere vapouring. On August 3rd 1914 he presented an urgent petition to his Majesty King Ludwig–III requesting to be allowed to serve in a Bavarian regiment and the next day his request was granted. Within few days he wore the uniform which he did not put off for six years. He was face to face with a mighty struggle and his past fell into oblivion. He was sent to fight at the front. Deaths began to make havoc in the ranks but he carried on to sing the song of valour. It was First World War. Fate might have put him through the final test without his nerves or reason giving away. Now the young volunteer had become an old soldier. The continuous fighting made him tough and hard to withstand all the assaults. But as per Hitler all the sacrifices came to naught and Germany was a Republic and he wept. He decided to join political work.

On the morning of 27th April 1919 he was to be arrested. But the three fellows did not dare and went back. He was invited to join German labour party but within, he wanted to form his own party. He brooded for two days over the offer and ultimately he decided to join the party with a heavy heart as he was not in a position to form his own party.

He was fully aware of the view that Jews were exploiting the German people but still he said,

> "The political leader should not estimate the worth of a religion by taking some of its shortcomings into account, but should ask himself whether there be any practical substitute in view of which is demonstrably better. Until such a substitute is available only fools and criminals would think of abolishing the existing religion. Undoubtedly, no small amount of blame for present unsatisfactory

religious situation must be attributed to those who have encumbered the ideal of religion with purely material accessories and have thus given rise to an utterly futile conflict between religion and science. In this conflict the victory will be on the side of science even though after a bitter struggle while religion will suffer heavily in the eyes of those who cannot penetrate beneath the mere superficial aspects of the science."

On the whole Hitler was deadly against the Jews. He said,

"Jews have no creative abilities which are necessary for founding the civilization. In them there is not and never has been that spirit of idealism which is an absolutely necessary element in the higher development of mankind. Therefore, the Jewish intellect will never be constructive but always destructive. Since the Jews have never had a state which was based on territorial delimitation and therefore never a civilization of their own – they are like nomads. The Aryan himself was probably at first a nomad and became a settler in course of ages. But yet he was never of the Jewish kind. A Jew is not a nomad, for a nomad has already a definite attitude towards the concept of work and this attitude served as the basis of a later cultural development. The Jews live the life of parasites thriving on the substance of other nations. Schopenhauer once described the Jew as 'the great master of lies'."

When one who had such a notion about Jews then it was but natural for him to punish them at the earliest occasion available. He was determined to set-up a German state in a German nation. But on the 9th of November 1923 the German Socialist Labour Party was dissolved and forbidden throughout the republic. But in 1926 it was again established enjoying full liberty, stronger and internally more compact than ever before. He was again determined,

"Germany must necessarily win the position which belongs to it on this earth if it is led and organized according to the principles unstrained in the party constitution. A state which in an epoch of racial adulteration, devotes itself to the duty of preserving the best

> of elements of its racial stock must one day become the ruler of the earth. The adherents of our movements must always remember this, whenever they may have misgivings lest the greatness of the sacrifices demanded of them may not be justified by the possibilities of success."

He was taught by Dr Jorg Lanz Van who stated that the world belonged to the fair skinned and the superior Aryan race, and all others belonged to sub-human culture.

World War I lasted from 1914 to 1918. The war totally changed the map of Europe. But it did not resolve all the issues that had caused it. Germany was defeated and the victors imposed severe penalties on the losers, leaving the economy of Germany in shambles. The people were left without jobs and its currency lost value. By the end of 1923 a loaf of bread cost 200 billion marks and the American dollar was worth more than one trillion marks. The Germans were left feeling humiliated and resentful.

Hitler had formally renounced his Austrian citizenship on 7 April 1925 but at the same time did not acquire German citizenship. He was a stateless person for seven years. Therefore, he was incapable to run for any public office. On 25 February 1932 the interior Minister of Brunswick who was member of NSDAP party appointed Hitler as administrator for the state's delegation to the Parliament in Berlin, making him a citizen of Brunswick and thus of Germany.

In 1932 he contested the election for President against Hindenburg. The viability of his candidacy was underscored by a speech on 27 January 1932 in the industry club Dusseldorf which won him support from various German industrialists. But he lost and was second with 35% but he established himself as a force in German politics. No effective government was likely to be formed. Therefore, the President elect thought fit to appoint Hitler Chancellor of the coalition government.

He declared that Germans were not a defeated nation in the World War I. They were actually the master race of Aryans – a pure race destined to rule the world. The Aryans need the living space to fulfil their destiny which was to create a great empire. After he became Chancellor, he tried to create absolute majority but he failed and Parliament was dissolved. Elections were held again and new Parliament was formed on 23rd March 1933. This day was celebrated as a day of unity between Nazi movement and the old Prussian elite and Military. He appeared in the morning coat and humbly greeted the President Hindenburg. He brought an Enabling Act in the house through which he got full legislative power for a period of four years. Ultimately, he secured absolute power and he removed the last legal remedy by which he could be removed from the office. He became the Supreme Commander of the armed forces because he was the head of the state. The traditional loyalty oath of the serviceman was altered to affirm loyalty to Hitler. He was made powerful through political and military power. In the meeting of his military officers, he spoke of Germanisation of East Europe in a ruthless way. His first conquest was Poland. In April 1940 Denmark was attacked and Norway followed and a month later, through Netherlands and Belgium, France was attacked. Nobody could resist him. The British army which had crossed into continental Europe to try to stop Nazi advance, retreated across the British channel. By the end of 1940 Hitler controlled most of the continental Europe and had begun bombing England. In 1941 he was moving against Yugoslavia and Greece. He violated the German treaty and launched a massive attack on Soviet Union. Hitler seemed unstoppable, at the same time Nazis began ridding Germany and other lands they have conquered, of various class of people they regarded as undesirable – above all Jews, mentally and physically disabled, homosexuals and political dissidents. As the persecution grew more and more intense, The Nazis began to talk of a final situation of the Jewish question – a horrendous plan to kill all European Jews.

But attack on Russia turned out to be a turning point in Hitler's for tunes. The battle for Stalingrad was the bloodiest in history. Both sides fought without carrying the cost and as a result 3 million soldiers and civilians were killed.

On June 6, 1944 D Day, the United States, Great Britain, Canada and France launched a huge offensive from the west. Germany was squeezed from all sides. In December 1944 Germany made a final effort to attack the Western Allies and to capture the port of Antwerp. But the US Third Army blocked the Germans in the battle of Bulge. At that time the Red Army was at the border of Germany.

In February 1945 the leaders of US, Great Britain and Soviet Union met at Yalta, on the Black Sea. Three unlikely allies, President Franklin D Roosevelt, Prime Minister Winston Churchill and Soviet leader Joseph Stalin made plans for a coordinated attack on Germany and agreed on the division of the country once defeated. The treaty known as Yalta Agreement, would have a profound impact on the lives of Germans in the decades to come.

In the spring of 1945, the Soviet army reached Berlin and on April 30, 1945, with his special underground bunker surrounded by Russian troops, Adolf Hitler killed himself. Before he killed himself he married his long time mistress Eva Braun. He had a public image of a celibate, a man without domestic life, dedicated entirely to his political mission and the nation.

The most significant work he did was the development of healthy people. He said,

> "Those who are physically and mentally unhealthy must not perpetuate their own sufferings in the bodies of their children. From the education point of view there is here a huge task for the people's state to accomplish. But in the future era this work will appear greater and more significant than the victorious wars of our present bourgeois epoch. Through education means the state must teach individuals that illness is not a disgrace but an unfortunate accident which has to be pitied, yet that is a crime and disgrace to make this affliction all the worse by passing on disease and defects to innocent creatures, out of mere egotism...."

If for a period of only 60 years those individuals would be sterilized who are physically degenerate or mentally diseased, humanity would not only be delivered from an immense misfortune but also restored to a state of general health such as we at present can hardly imagine. If the fecundity of the healthy portion of the nation should be made a practical matter in a conscientious and methodical way, we should have at least the beginnings of a race from which all those germs would be eliminated which are today the cause of our moral and physical decadence. If the people and the state take this course to develop that nucleus of the nation which is most valuable from the racial standpoint and thus increase its fecundity the people as a whole will subsequently enjoy that most precious gifts which consists in a racial quality fashioned on truly noble lines. He made the beginning and we see the result when we look to the German people.

By sheer determination and hard struggle he became the overall master of Germany. After driving out the Jews to Austria, he had to wage a constant war for taking his country out of the clutches of the Jews. He did not rest on this success. Now he struggled to take revenge for the excesses the Jews did to the German people. A very strong army was prepared. He talked to the dictator of Italy, Mussolini and later on to Hirohito of Japan and forged an alliance of power to wage a war against the rest of Europe and South-West Asia.

By his strong vocal appeal to his countrymen, he exhorted the people to stand up and fight for the dignity of Germany. His people stood with him and not only the army but the Navy and Air strike was sharpened as per the need of the adventure. But the Jews did not do the front fighting, they prepared an atom bomb with the help of USA. That bomb reversed the whole game. Japan went out of war. This weakness encouraged the discouraged Churchill.

Even a street dog manages its food but the great persons care for others and they benefit millions. Hitler was a great person because he took out his whole nation out of sufferings political social and religious. He himself suffered greatly. He did manual labour. He was put to prisons. But he did not waiver, with every strike on him he rose stronger and to the extent that the whole world took note of him and shuddered at his very name. Really, he was made of steel and his mind was a super computer and he wanted to set his nation on these lines – healthy people with quite healthy minds who do not waiver with the flicker of occasion. He was a great genius of history. His political ideals, his beliefs and his motivation shall be remembered for a very long time to come. About the power and brutal treatment during his years of power he himself said, "cruelty impresses, the people want to be afraid of something. They want someone to whom they can submit with a shudder, The masses need that. They need something to dread."

He will go down in the history of world, a person who lived on his own terms. When he failed to dictate, he went from the scene not to face disgrace, which was not in his blood.

Historian Meanceke described Hitler as one of the great examples of singular and incalculable power of personality in historical life. English historian T Repar saw Hitler as a simplifier of history, the most systematic, the most historical, the most philosophical and yet the coarsest conqueror of the world ever known. Hitler married his mistress Eva Braun just one day before his death. He had no issues. He had his half niece Gali Raubal who also committed suicide with Hitler's gun in his Munich apartment. Her death gave him great pain. Paula Hitler was the last living member of his immediate family who died in 1960.

Fidel Castro

FIDEL CASTRO was born on 13 August 1926 in the Orients in Cuba. His father was a prosperous sugar and timber man. He went to a Catholic School, the first in Santiago de Cuba, a big town in the Orients. From here he went to a Jesuit High school in Havana and then to Havana university to be a lawyer. He became a lawyer in 1950. He had a very busy practice in Havana itself. But he was not like other lawyers. He worked for poor people and political prisoners. He was becoming more revolutionary.

Let us talk a bit briefly about the condition of Cuba at that time and earlier. Cuba is an island near USA, only 90 miles away. They say it is a part of Latin America. It was under Spain and later on it was taken over by the dictator Batista. The tourists from outside Cuba used to come here, specially to Havana, the capital city of the island. Some tourists used to lie down in the sun on the Cuban beaches where Cubans were not allowed. Cubans call these Europeans Yankee. Havana was a gambling haven and a whoring station. In Havana, there was big money for few people and Cubans were used to beg from these outsiders. Here, girls of 12 and 14 years old and fresh from their bohios were called here for sin. A lot of that gambling money ended up in the pockets of corrupt government officers. Also much of it ended in the pockets of their gangsters from Chicago, New York and Los Angeles. The money also ended up in the pockets of the touts working there. No one knows, how many girls and women were whores in Cuba during the last years of the Batista tyranny. In Havana before the downfall of the tyranny there were some 270 over crowded brothels. There were hotel and motel renting rooms at hour basis for this purpose. There were 700 bars congested with hostesses – the first step. Before prostitution there were about 12 meseras to each bar at the rate of 2 dollars per day but the grafter got 52 dollars a day. There was no record of the gambling dens. But it was a thorough and complete racket directly under the tyranny of the big men.

The government of dictator Batista was recognized by USA in 1933 and he ruled Cuba with a very strong hand with the help of the army, which was trained and supported by USA. They say 20,000 Cubans were murdered. Any one who dared to oppose was a dirty communist and was tortured, mutilated and killed. Batista was a barbarian and cruel savage with lethal weapons and modern torture at his command. In Havana itself, many boys and men were castrated and when women were raped their husbands were made to look upon it. The police stations were the torture chambers.

His bully boys were everywhere, kicking, stealing, arresting, smashing and the excuse was: The dirty Communists, they are trying to take over the fine democracy.

Fidel Castro was a lawyer. He was helping the poor litigants. When Batista took over Cuba and the days of tyranny started, Castro could not tolerate it. He was burnt from within. He decided to get rid of this tyrant. He collected 172 young men and two girls for this purpose. They attacked the Batista garrison in Moncade in 1953. Batista proclaimed that Castro was killed in the attack. All of them turned revolutionaries. But Castro was not satisfied. He wanted a full force to drive out Batista from Cuba.

He escaped to Mexico for military training. He returned to Cuba in Orient in the year 1956. He arranged guns. These guns, they say were guns from USA. But how did these guns fall into the hands of Castro? It was a simple affair. USA had provided weapons to Batista in the guise of protecting the Hemisphere from the communists effect. These guns were provided to gangsters by Batista. But one night, up an alley, in a town four of Castro's men jumped over Batista's men and killed them and snatched the guns. Thus, started the game of Castro as he arranged the needed weapons.

In the same province, Orient in which Castro lived, there was a woman in Santiago de Cuba. She was educated and was in her forties. Her house was up in the mountains. During the day Batista's soldiers came there and during the night these rebels, the men of Castro used to come there. But she was with Castro. She turned revolutionary. She was from Manzanillo from where many rebels came.

But the real revolution began when Castro came back from Mexico in 1956. Everybody knew that he had come and he was not killed as Batista said earlier. In that period of three years, every day somebody was killed. Although the Batista Government was recognized by USA yet Castro submitted a memorandum against this reorganization but Batista threw it away and said "I am the Government." Still Castro said, "You are not the Government." He sued him in court and said that Batista Government had violated the law. But the petition was thrown away. After his military training in Mexico he met Che Guevara and others. Their number was 82 and they got on to a small yacht and came to invade Cuba. It was another disaster, this time worse than Moncada. They got lost, they missed their connection with the men waiting for them in Cuba. They bogged down in a terrible shore swamp, they were attacked. It ended with just 12 men on the top of the mountain. To these 12 persons Castro said, "The days of Batista are numbered." Now everybody knows that Castro was right at that time.

This prompted many students and intellectuals to be with these revolutionaries. But intelligentsia split into two. Many sided with the tyranny. Many left Cuba. But the men of Castro were made of steel and said, "We have no God who failed." They did not have cynicism and futility about what they were doing and about what they felt.

There was a clear difference between what Batista was doing in Cuba and what these revolutionaries guided by Fidel Castro were aiming at. The revolutionaries of Castro were from the middle class – not the peasants or labourers who are very easily bought. Every revelation exaggerates the evil of the old order. But Cubans had not done so. In its realities, the rural order of the old Cuba was an exaggeration – an exaggeration of social hell. It was a place of unrelieved poverty without any hope. Before, when Castro's revolutionaries were making the insurrection, they did not know everything about this. The one thing they knew was the result of all this and that was easy to see: Poverty. This poverty was the settled condition, felt personally as total absence of any future. Every year to this rural misery and sloth came the dead season, and then the field hands and mill workers were hungry. Because of the short season of work in the fields, the sugar mills and because sugar was a dominating crop and nothing was done about it Cubans were without work for months. The Cuban revolution was not based on the economic order. The result of that economy and abject poverty was the real cause of action for Castro. And he was able to organise the people from top to bottom. The leaders of the Castro revolution were young intellectuals and students of Havana University. They were the pioneers who made the first move. The fight was against the trained army of Batista. They had good supplies of every need. About 7 months before the final strike on Batista, there was a strike in the city and that failed. The failure was due to the fact that the forces of tyranny were turned against the revolutionaries in the mountains. Those forces were taken to the mountains to kill the revolutionaries once and for all. Castro had only 300. Thirteen army teams each 900 man strong, came towards the mountains. These 12,000 men, fully trained, the biggest troop, movement in truck, jeeps. Sharman tanks supplied by Yankees – USA, clanked towards the mountain. Castro's men waited for them in logs and earth bunkers. Castro's people dug traps, blew up bridges on highways and hid in trees to snipe in jungle on cliffs up the gorges. They dropped the napalm bombs supplied by USA. Then the troops moved to the jungle. But revolutionaries were certainly good shooters. Batista's forces got tired quickly. They were flabby and could not shoot worth of a damn. The officers were plain stupids. They did not have iron faces but had wooden heads. They also brought bazookas but these were shot at and captured. The Castro people captured their tanks when their troops fled abandoning them in the gasoline fired tank traps fixed along the rail. Their radio and code book was captured. Their supply lines were cut-off. Over their own radio the Castro people misled them fully and their own troops were finished.

Their plans and parachutes were with revolutionaries. These revolutionaries ate up their meat from cans which these people had not tasted for months. Therefore, there is a story of insurrection in one sentence: A handful of men on a mountain top, half starving at that, defeated 12,000 men army paid and fed by Batista the tyrant and backed by a big force of the world, the USA. No one paid the revolutionaries. But they had a big objective that went beyond their personal interest. They represented Cuba so they won.

There were scenes of Cubans shooting Cubans. 500-600 Batistas were executed. This was the war against Batista who killed thousands Cubans. Then what can be expected against that tyrant? At this Castro uttered Remember Yankees, that morals are easy to come by sitting in your quiet suburbs away from it all, protected from it all. Morals are easy to say out when you are rich and strong and all the unpleasantness of the world is hidden from you by distance, by amusement, by your own indifference, by your own private way of life. The history of Castro's Cuba is really cruel because injustices are very hard to remove. By the execution of worst, Batista hoodlums and putting the others in jails, Fidel Castro's soldiers saved Cuba from further blood bath. It was announced on radio act with revolutionary restraint, "You will have justice." If he had not done that Cuba would have been witnessed a blood bath.

This ensured that some of the businessmen of Cuba went against Fidel Castro. There is a counter revolutionary theme song all over the business song. What does it all mean? This means that Castro's revolution has been shown in their business books. The Cubans wanted nice, safe and bit little democracy, devoid of the Yankees. This prompted the organized propaganda against Castro and his way of handling the affairs of his country. So long as Batista ruled, there were no protests of his tyrannies and bloodbath woos, in USA and elsewhere. They supplied guns, planted bombs and trained the Batistas to use them against the Cubans. At that time, no one protested. What kind of justice is this? But Cubans were overjoyed when Batista was defeated although the Radios of Yankees had all the time to denounce Fidel Castro and his Cuba. But all this made Castro strong and more determined to set everything right, distorted by Batista.

They say every revolution has its counter revolution – that is the sure sign of real revolution – therefore it becomes the duty of the revolutionaries to defeat the counter revolution. These counter revolutions are always supported from abroad. But Castro defended Cuba well, against those who went out of Cuba for fear of execution against their crimes perpetuated on the innocent people of Cuba for their business ends.

These elements have plenty of money which they stole from Cuba. By dint of this money power they thought that they would be successful in their counter revolution. But they had no force inside Cuba. Here Castro regime had formed the congressional committees. But the system they defend was so drenched with blood, crimes against poverty that they cannot gain any support here in these committees. Still dozen of persons sitting out of Cuba made every effort to defeat the revolution. They were people like Huber Matos – once a commandant who fought with fidel at the mountains, Diaz Lanz head of the Batista air force, Raul Chibas brother of Edurdo Chibas and Luis Agirero, a radioman settled at Miami. They may have lot of money in the banks but counter revolution requires the zeal, determination, pure inner will and the welfare of the people. They deserted Fidel because their properties were taken by the administration with the force of the law made for the people of Cuba. Some properties of the family of Castro have also been acquired by the administration. At that Castro did not intervene. He stood holding the balance of justice – each and every one according to the law. The opposition of French and Chinese revolutions persisted for many years but here inside Cuba everything settled very quickly.

In the beginning, some people inside Cuba had the murmuring voice against the revolution. They were the people who were benefited from the old regime but not from the revolution. Most of the big Cuban landowners have been affected by the land laws and their surplus land gone out of their hands, certainly gone to those who did not have it. Such beneficiaries are large in number. Therefore, the murmuring voices didn't come out in the open anymore. A person shifted to Miami from Cuba described the revolution like this:

> "At first I was all for Castro. True, I did not get the gun to fight alongside him, that was not his job. But still was glad he was winning. But now I am against him and his revolution he is making in Cuba. He has gone too far, much too far. In Cuba they call me counter-revolutionary, and perhaps I am, except, I had much rather say that I am for true revolution, therefore I am against what Fidel is doing and what his bearded men are doing. Old Cuba was really a bad place. Fidel was right about it. Yet somehow, despite everything they may say, I like it. A man could make plenty of money there and spend it well too."

Now is the question: "Is present Cuba not better than the old Cuba?"

The revolution in Cuba was a moment of political truth and here are some points of political truth.

Under a tyranny, all politics of any consequence are politics of guerrilla. Under condition of poverty all politics of any consequence are politics of economic construction.

Under conditions of ignorance, all politics of any consequences are the politics of educational construction.

By the military and then by economic and the educational efforts, the Cubans threw away politics and that did not remain there under Castro.

First, in a military moment and then in economic and education moment all politics becomes irrelevant and everything becomes political. That is the political truth about Cuba and it is not a paradox. The old politics they had done away with – that was the politics of the thief and exploiter and the new politics in is the politics of the construction of a new social order.

Everyone who was even half honest became honest on two points: Before the revolution Cuba was a land of grief, fear and frequent horror and under Castro the people became enormously happy. No one dreamed of such a miracle. No one thought that such a complete power would not immediately corrupt the men.

The reconstruction that Cuba started so soon could not be imagined by the people. Castro was with few ill equipped rebels and they defeated Batista, large and well equipped battalions. Thereafter Castro started building these rebels a new type of militia.

Thousands of acres of land was waste but thereafter it went under economic use.

Starting with illiteracy and dreadful lack of education at all levels Castro made a new education system from kindergarten to university. The government worked full day and half the night and all Cubans worked for it, willingly, enthusiastically. The people were filled with hope.

Castro's men are working without any hampering at any stage and people gained confidence that this is the government which will work for them – they are not thieves and dishonest thugs – Castro gave full liberty to the people and the people said – It is the real liberty. The people really worked and did the simple taking. Now politics of half truths went out of Cuba and the people had faith in the system of the government working in the country. They became fully confident about the working of Castro's system of governance. The people became responsible to themselves, to the country and to Castro.

At the time of revolution there was enough restrictions, laziness and stereo types. Castro told the country to smash it and today after half a century these bad elements are hard to be seen in Cuba. He opened up the free society. He prepared a seed bed on which no laziness could grow. Only sharp brains grew, which did not create problems but solved the existing problems. There is such a university in the capital city of Havana which has worldwide faculties where China's communist scholar discusses with a north American Republican Party member freely about the world affairs – the meaning of freedom, world economy and social order, a Polish scholar discusses with another Venezuelan scholar the issues of collectivization, where British Labour Party member discusses with a Yugoslav politician whatever issue he desires to discuss. All these discussions are on print and are published in newspapers. These are included in the books. Nothing is left concealed and everything is in the open. It is a very open society with open thinking and open living encompassing entire range of world opinion, study, art and judgement. They say that Yankees are afraid of communists because universities in Russia and China are not open.

Castro's fight with USA turned into the cold war between Russia and USA. In addition to UNO the whole world always heard about the tension of two super powers. Russia was planning to have its war base in Cuba and USA was always against it. This wordy warfare went on till Russia disintegrated. In the mean time, Castro had consolidated his hegemony over the island very well. The people there took him as their emancipator who was earlier leading a dreadful life under the stooge of USA, Batista.

The world stood on the brink of Armageddon for 13 days in October 1962 when President Kennedy drew a symbolic line in the Atlantic and warned of the consequences if Nikita Khrushchev, the then head of Soviet Russia, crossed the line. An American U-2, a sky plane flying high over Cuba had snapped aerial photographs of Soviet ballistic missiles sites that could launch war heads with little warning at the US just 90 miles away. It was the height of the cold war and many people feared a nuclear war would annihilate human civilization. The Soviet ships carrying nuclear equipments steamed toward Kennedy's quarantine zone around the Island but turned around before reaching the line eyeball to eyeball and where other follow just blinked. It was the bold brinkmanship of Kennedy which averted the crisis. They also say that it was behind the scenes compromise rather than a high stakes game of chicken that resolved the face off, that both Washington and Moscow wound up winners and that the crisis lasted for longer than 13 days.

Declassified documents, oral histories and accounts from decision-makers involved in the standoff have turned up new information that scholar say, provides lessons for leaders embroiled in such crisis.

But it was the wisdom of Castro which did not allow Russia to be much involved in the internal affairs of his country. He did take the help but without any string attached to it. He by dint of his own wisdom and self-training turned the people of the island to be so faithful to their country and their leader that any sort of outside greed, mistracking and allurement could not sake them a bit out of the set line of working with self-confidence and self-respect. Really, it is a matter of great appreciation that a mighty power at the door utterly failed to sabotage the programme set forth by Fidel Castro after dedicatedly following his conscience to take his people out of slavery, poverty and tyranny.

Fidel Castro is now 86 year old. He had been at the helm of affairs of his country for the last 50 years. This is half a century. During such a long period there came many strong pulls and pushes which can shake a person how so ever strong he may be, out of power. But this giant in flesh and blood stood against a giant country on the door of his country, like a colossal without any harm to his country rather he made many strides in progress in all spheres. Economically, Cuba is far ahead of other south American countries. There per capita income has increased manifold in comparison to the time when Castro returned from Mexico and undertook to liberate Cuba. Educationally, Cuba sits with her head high in the galaxy of well advanced countries. Socially, the island is fully integrated and all sections of society pine for the welfare of their country without any ill will towards any other section of the society.

Now, Castro has transferred his ruling powers to his younger brother Raul and he sits like a mature guiding force to him. It is two years but his people respect him like before. His esteem has increased due to the transfer of power without being asked by anyone. Such bold, intelligent and strong willed persons are rarely seen in the world.

USA is giant and Cuba is just like a mole before it. The question was how to survive against this giant. Fidel Castro managed Cuban affairs in such a way that Cuba not only survived but flourished to a great extent – simply 90 miles away, the giant country tried to finish Cuba – by economic bans, by military threats, by sending sabotagers in Cuba, by destroying their social order, by alluring Cuban intellectuals and last but not the least by branding Cuba a stooge of Russia – a communist agent. But Castro stood like a rock and withstood every hard push and a very strong pull. He made his programme to rebuilt Cuba in a way to erase the tyranny of Batista from the minds of his people and set the new generation on the road of reconstruction. It is not a year, it is not a decade, it is the half a century when Castro threw away Batista, a stooge of USA – the giant, and Cubans can really boast of everything new in their country, without any outside support economic or otherwise.

There have been a number of strong men in history but Fidel Castro is unique among them. He had been standing erect for half a century against the super power of the world and has made his country well advanced from land fully plundered and butchered by Batista, courtesy USA. Really, Fidel Castro is a great person of the world.

Subhas Chandra Bose

SUBHAS CHANDRA BOSE was born on 23 January 1897 at Cuttak in India. His father was Janki Dass Bose. At that time, the British Empire was celebrating Golden Jubilee of Queen Victoria's reign in India and was at its Zenith. He was a deeply interpretive child with a profourd emotional frame of mind. Awakening was taking shape in Bengal, creating great turbulence. In the entire social fabric young minds were stirred and roused. There was political awareness and national consolidation in India. Subhas was moved up to the bones by the sad plight of the country under British rule. The unusual thing about him was that he understood and perceived the historic destiny of Indians and his inborn faith led him to discover the divinity in his mother land. When he was only 15, he wrote to his mother, "India is God's own beloved land." He has been born in this great land in every age in the form of a saviour for enlightenment of the people to rid this earth of its sins and to establish righteousness." He once again wrote to her, "Mother, I wonder, if mother India in this age, has one single selfless son. Where are those Aryans heroes who would freely sacrifice their precious lives on mother India?"

Direct experience of abject social, economic, cultural and political conditions of his people gradually matured his mind and gave a more positive direction to his sense of mission and nationalism. A study of the emasculating effects of the long colonial subjugation of his people led him to ponder deeply over the priorities for a national worker. Even so when he decided to set sail for England to qualify for Indian Civil Service in 1919, he had yet to resolve within himself the conflict between expediency and principle. The Indian Civil Service brought him face-to-face with the first major ideological challenge in his life. The rising tides of nationalism into which he was born, demanded that he made his choice between expediency and principle once and for all. He rose to the occasion and wrote to his elder brother, Sarat Chandra, to justify his decision of resigning from the Indian Civil Service,

> "We who have grown under the influence of Swami Vivekananda and Aurobindo Ghose have developed a mentality which does not accept a compromise. Under the present circumstances should we own allegiance to a foreign bureaucracy and sell ourselves for mess of pottage?"

For him Indian Civil Service was simply a mess of pottage. He added,

> "we have not come to that stage where we can accept a philosophy of expediency. We have got to make a nation and the nation can be made only by uncompromising idealism of Hampden and Cromwell. The first step was to sacrifice all worldly interests. A life of sacrifice, of sufferings or even of poverty, is heartily welcome to me if only it is in the interest of our national cause. Let the money spent on me as a gift laid out at the feet of mother without any expectation or return in any shape or form."

Even without meeting his would be Guru, Deshbandhu Chittaranjan Das, he wrote to him, "I am now ready, you have only to command me to go into action."

He returned to India from Cambridge, England in the middle of 1921 and was full of self confidence and unreservedly committed to the national cause. He placed himself fully in the lap of Deshbandhu Chittaranjan Das. He once said about his leader,

> "If one fails to identify one's own life with the life of the nation, one can not realise what is patriotism. A man in whom patriotism is aroused as a result of identification of his own life with that of nation, he can find a new identification and can create a new nation. The fundamental truth is all Sadhana – complete control of limbs, is to be completely absorbed in the idea to be inspired totally by the same idea in life, death, sleep and dreams – they become one."

He met Deshbandhu Chittaranjan Das in July 1921 and placed his total self to him and sought his guidance for the work to be done for the nation. They also discussed Gandhi and his way of working. Both were not satisfied with the way of his working. They decided to adopt a tough stance against, the Britishers. Keeping the youth of the country in view, he issued a statement:

> "The kind of freedom you demand, without which life is utterly meaningless and to gain which we have been shedding our blood cheerfully, that freedom is in every sphere and field of life. Be it sociology, economics, politics or either, we want to bring the light of truth, upsurge of Anand (supreme pleasure), and fundamentals of liberalism."

He again said,

> "The Indian nation has passed through so many deaths and resurrections and that is because of the fact that it has a mission and its civilization has a purpose that has yet not fulfilled. Only that Indian who believes in the mission of India is really alive, as the youths of India have the faith in the mission of India so they are truly alive."

The mission that Subhas was preaching was an all consuming one and admitted no retreat and compromise. Those who want to create a new

India have only to renounce to sacrifice throughout their lives to give themselves away fully and become paupers without asking anything in return. "Life will attain real fulfilment on the basis of total sacrifice of the life." Therefore he, in his life never accepted any policy or proposition of his reason or conscience did not approve of them.

The Britishers were so afraid of him that he was exiled in Burma-Myanmar, for four years 1924-27. But, there in prison he transformed as a leader from a mere rebel. He was fully prepared for the task ahead. Deep introspection and meaningful studies in loneliness added maturity of Judgement to the buoyancy and revolutionary spirit of this youth. He had a conviction that even in non-violent struggle for independence, the fighting forces had to be organised on basically the same model and under the same rules, discipline as in armed battle. This was more necessary when our people had to face the might of the British Empire. He gave a demonstration of battle dress at the Kolkata Session of Congress in 1928.

When Gandhi moved a resolution of Dominion Status as the goal of Congress, Subhas moved the amendment of full freedom.

He had a deep emotional attachment to the national revolutionary elements in the country for their idealism and deathless courage, burning patriotism and sense of sacrifice regardless of the methods or meanings of struggle against the alien power. He believed that these forces in the truly historical sense, were very much part of the national movement and integral to it.

He had to suffer long terms of imprisonment – eleven times, during the course of his tumultuous life. It was he who taught the Indian to look ahead without British views.

He forged the links of lasting friendships and understanding with central Europe and desired that free India should have an open mind and a broad view to as world events and world history.

Taking into consideration his bright personality, he was called to preside over the Congress session in 1938 – yes, the Congress which was formed by a Britisher, Indian Civil Service Officer, HO Hume as a His Majesty's organisation to 'oppose' his government. He said that Indian nationalism and British Imperialism were irreconcilable and no compromise between them is possible. He also said that Congress should function as a broad anti-imperialist front including in its fold the workers, the peasants, the youth, students and all other patriotic elements of Indian society cutting across all sectarian and communal antagonisms.

Thus, there arose the differences between him and the party leadership on the assessment of the national situation, interpretation of international events, our socio-economic goals and methods of struggle. But Subhas in a buoyant mood cared little for an outmoded and limping policy of the old person who throughout gave in before those who were to be taken out of the country. He was for striking at the red hot iron but Gandhi was for wait and watch as their own man. This policy was tested and failed.

A new President was to come in his place. Since 1885, no one presided immediately the next time. But Subhas was chosen despite the stiff opposition of Gandhi. All progressive elements in the Congress supported him, even Jawaharlal Nehru, the disciple of Gandhi. But Gandhi put obstacles in his smooth functioning.

Addressing the Congress Session of the Indian National Congress at Tripuri in the year 1939 he said:

> "Chairman, sister and brother delegates! I thank you from the bottom of my heart for the great honour you have done me by re-electing me to the Presidential chair of the Indian National Congress and also for the warm and cordial welcome you have given me here at Tripuri. It is true that at my request you have had to dispense with some of the pomp that is usual on such occasions; but I feel that enforced step has not taken away one iota of the warmth and cordiality of your reception and I hope that nobody will regret the curtailment of it on this occasion."

He was seriously ill at the time of this session of the Congress and he was elected for a second time despite the tooth and nail opposition of Mohandas Karamchand Gandhi. He was running 107 degree fever, the address was read by his brother:

> "Friends, before I proceed any further, I shall voice your feelings by expressing our joy at the success of Mahatma Gandhi's mission to Rajkot and the termination of his fast in consequence thereof.
>
> Friends, this year promises to be an abnormal or extraordinary one in many ways. The Presidential election this time was not of the humdrum type. The election was followed by sensational developments culminating in the resignation of twelve out of fifteen members of the Working Committee, headed by Sardar Vallabhbhai Patel, Maulana Abul Kalam Azad and Dr Rajendra Prasad. Another distinguished and eminent member of the Working Committee, Pandit Jawaharlal Nehru, though he did not formally resign, issued a statement which led everybody to believe that he had also resigned. On the eve of the Tripuri Congress, events at Rajkot forced Mahatma Gandhi to undertake a vow of fast unto death. And then the President arrived at Tripuri, a sick man. It will, therefore, be in the fitness of things if the Presidential address this year can claim to be a departure from precedent in the matter of its length.
>
> Since we met at Haripura in February, 1938, several significant events have taken place in the international sphere. The most important of these is the Munich Pact of September, 1939, which implied an abject surrender to Nazi Germany on the part of the Western Powers, France and Great Britain. As a result of this, France ceased to be the dominant power in Europe and the hegemony passed into the hands of Germany without a shot being fired. In more recent times, the gradual collapse of the Republican Government in Spain seems to have added to the strength and prestige of Fascist Italy and Nazi Germany. The so-called democratic powers, France and Great Britain, have joined Italy

and Germany in conspiring to eliminate Soviet Russia from European politics, for the time being. But how long will that be possible?

There is no doubt, that as a result of recent international developments, in Europe as well as in Asia, British and French Imperialism have received a considerable setback in the matter of strength and prestige.

Coming to home politics, in view of my ill-health, I shall content myself with referring to only a few important problems. In the first place, I must give clear and unequivocal expression to what I have been feeling for some time past, namely, that the time has come for us to raise the issue of Swaraj and submit our national demand to the British Government in the form of an ultimatum. The time is long past when we could have adopted a passive attitude and waited for the Federal scheme to be imposed on us. The problem no longer is as to when the Federal scheme will be forced down our throats. The problem is as to what we should do if the Federal scheme is conveniently shelved for a few years till peace is stabilized in Europe. There is no doubt that once there is stable peace in Europe, whether through a Four Power Pact or through some other means, Great Britain will adopt a strong Empire policy. The fact that she is now showing some signs of trying to conciliate the Arabs as against the Jews in Palestine is because she is feeling herself weak in the international sphere. In my opinion, therefore, we should submit our national demand to the British Government in the form of an ultimatum and give a certain time-limit within which a reply is to be expected. If no reply is received within this period or if an unsatisfactory reply is received, we should resort to such sanctions as we possess in order to enforce our national demand.

The sanctions that we posses today are mass civil disobedience or Satyagraha. And the British Government today is not in a position to face a major conflict like an All-India Satyagraha for a long period. It grieves me to find that there are people in the Congress who are so pessimistic as to think that the time is not ripe for a major assault on British Imperialism. But looking at the situation in a thoroughly realistic manner, I do not see the slightest ground for pessimism. With Congress in power in eight provinces, the strength and prestige of our national organisation has gone up. The mass movement has made considerable headway throughout British India. And last but not the least, there is an unprecedented awakening in the Indian States. What more opportune moment could we find in our national history for a final advance in the direction of Swaraj, particularly when the international situation is favourable to us? Speaking as a cold-blooded realist, I may say that all the facts of the present day situation are so much to our advantage that one should entertain the highest degree of optimism. If only we sink our differences, pool all our resources and pull our full weight in the national struggle, we can make our attack on British Imperialism irresistible. Shall we have the political foresight to make the most of our present favourable position or shall we miss this opportunity, which is a rare opportunity in the lifetime of a nation?

I have referred earlier to the advisability of our making a final advance in the direction of Swaraj. That will need adequate preparation. In the first place, we shall have to take steps to ruthlessly remove whatever corruption or weakness has entered our ranks largely due to the lure of power. Next, we shall have to work in close cooperation with all anti-imperialist organisations in the country particularly the Kisan movement and the Trade Union movement. All the radical elements in the country must work in close harmony and cooperation and the efforts of all anti-imperialist organisations must converge in the direction of a final assault on British Imperialism.

Friends, today the atmosphere within the Congress is clouded and dissensions have appeared. Many of our friends are

> consequently feeling depressed and dispirited. The cloud that you see today is a passing one. I have faith in the patriotism of my countrymen and I am sure that before long we shall be able to tide over the present difficulties and restore unity within our ranks. A somewhat similar situation had arisen at the time of the Gaya Congress in 1922 and thereafter, when Deshbandhu Das and Pandit Motilal Nehru, of hallowed memory, started the Swarajya Party. May the spirit of my late Guru, of revered Motilalji and of other great sons of India inspire us in the present crisis and may Mahatma Gandhi, who is still with us to guide and assist our nation, help the Congress out of the present tangle is my earnest prayer. Vande Mataram."

But Gandhi adopted the adamant attitude and did not allow Subhas Chandra Bose to work. All the appeals of Subhas went futile and a golden opportunity to liberate India was lost due to ego of Mahatma. He resigned and left Gandhi's Congress – Yes the Congress President of which, even once was chosen from London, because Congress was being brooded by the empire and Gandhi was a part of the machinery. Gandhi was playing His Majesty's opposition and Subhas was in favour of taking the Britishers out of India. Both were carrying out their work quite sincerely.

Subhas was consigned to house arrest. He preferred to be lonely there. He grew a long beard and after some time sneaked out of the country in the guise of a Pathan – as habitant of a neighbouring country. The World War was on at that time. Hitler was defeating the whole of Europe. France and Austria were almost subjugated and Britain was jittery. Therefore, Subhas thought fit to work with Hitler to take the Britishers out of India. He met Hitler and both decided that Subhas should work with Japan and face the Britishers at Burma front. He travelled in a torpedo with a risk to his life because there was heavy bombardment by the enemy over the sea. He reached Japan and signed an agreement to fight with Japan against the Britishers on Burma front.

He organized the Indian National Army (INA) and also established the Indian Government in Singapore. Indian prisoners of wars from the British army were part of INA. A women regiment was also formed under the Command of Laxmi Sehgal. He himself took the command of the Indian National Army which was sent on the Burma Front. While addressing the Indians in Singapore he exerted them to donate maximum for the Indian Army. The people donated with open hearts. The garlands offered to him were put to auction. These also brought a very handsome amount. Once he said, "Give me blood, I will give you the freedom." At this the youth offered their services in the Indian National Army. The dream which Subhas saw transformed into reality. He got required number of recruits and the money for the expenses there upon. At many places he was weighed with costly ornaments offered by the Indian women on the spot. He was also weighed in silver coins by the Indian traders because he had exerted them for patriotism. He used to say, "The day on which we shall unfurl the tricolour on Red Fort of Delhi is not for off. Mother India is calling us. Therefore let us go to Delhi."

While reviewing the Indian National Army he said:

> "Soldiers of India's Army of Liberation! Today is the proudest day of my life. Today, it has pleased Providence to give me the unique privilege and honour of announcing to the whole world that India's Army of Liberation has come into being. This army has now been drawn up in military formation on the battlefield of Singapore – which was once the bulwark of the British Empire. This is not only the army that will emancipate India from the British yoke, it is also the army that will hereafter, create the future national army of Free India. Every Indian must feel proud that this army – his own army – has been organised entirely under Indian leadership and that when the historic moment arrives, under Indian leadership it will go to battle.... Standing today on the graveyard of the British empire, even a child is convinced that the almighty British empire is already a thing of the past.
>
> When France declared war on Germany in 1939 and the campaign began, there was but one cry which rose from the lips of

the German soldiers – 'To Paris, To Paris!' When the brave soldiers of Nippon set out on their march in December 1941 there was but one cry which rose from their lips – 'To Singapore, to Singapore!' Comrades! Soldiers! Let your battle-cry be – 'To Delhi, To Delhi!' How many of us will individually survive this war of freedom, I do not know. But I do know this, that we shall ultimately win and our task will not end until our surviving heroes hold the victory parade on another graveyard of the British empire – the Lal Qila or Red Fortress of ancient Delhi….

Let me remind you that you have a two-fold task to perform. With the force of arms and at the cost of your blood you will have to win liberty. Then, when India is free, you will have to organise the permanent army of Free India, whose task it will be to preserve our liberty for all time. We must build our national defence on such an unshakable foundation that never again in our history shall we lose our freedom.

As soldiers, you will always have to cherish and live up to the three ideals of faithfulness, duty and sacrifice. Soldiers who always remain faithful to their nation, who are always prepared to sacrifice their lives, are invincible. If you, too, want to be invincible, engrave these three ideals in the innermost core of your hearts

To those of you who are officers, I should like to say that your responsibility is a heavy one. Though the responsibility of an officer in every army in this world is indeed great, it is far greater in your case. Because of our political enslavement, we have no tradition like that of Mukden, Port Arthur or Sedan to inspire us. We have to unlearn some of the things that the British taught us and we have to learn much that they did not teach. Nevertheless, I am confident that you will rise to the occasion and fulfil the task that your countrymen have thrown on your brave shoulders. Remember always, that officers can make or unmake an army. Remember too, that the British have suffered defeats on so many fronts largely because of worthless officers. And remember also, that out of your ranks will be born the future General Staff of the Army of Free India.

Comrades! You have voluntarily accepted a mission that is the noblest that the human mind can conceive of. For the fulfilment of such a mission no sacrifice is too great, not even the sacrifice of one's life. You are today the custodians of India's national honour and the embodiment of India's hopes and aspirations. So conduct yourself that your, countrymen may bless you and posterity may be proud of you.

I have said that today is the proudest day of my life. For an enslaved people, there can be no greater pride, no higher honour, than to be the first soldier in the army of liberation. But this honour carries with it a corresponding responsibility and I am deeply conscious of. I assure you that I shall be with you in darkness and in sunshine, in sorrow and in joy, in suffering and in victory. For the present, I can offer you nothing except hunger, thirst, privation, forced marches and death. But if you follow me in life and in death, as I am confident you will, I shall lead you to victory and freedom. It does not matter who among us will live to see India free. It is enough that India shall be free and that we shall give our all to make her free. May God now bless our Army and grant us victory in the coming fight! Inquilab Zindabad! Azad Hind Zindabad!"

INA fought very bravely at every front despite shortages of weapons and food supplies. The troops were near Kohima in India and they were fighting hungry for the three days and British troops were retreating speedily. But unfortunately, USA bombarded Hiroshima and Nagasaki of Japan with atom bombs and as a result Japan declared ceasefire and the war ended. Thus, Subhas could not succeed in his mission to get India free.

But this fearless struggle of Subhas and the uprising in the British army in India constrained England to see the bleak future of their rule in India. They were wise enough to leave India before they were turned out by force and disgracefully.

It was the design of Subhas and his undoubting mission to take the Britishers out of India even at the cost of his own life. It was his organisational skill which brought Hitler and Japan to his help. It was his determination and love for the motherland that thousands of war prisoners took a leaf from his life and fought for the freedom of their motherland instead of for those who were ruling over them.

They say after Japan's ceasefire Subhas was offered safe passage to some unknown place. It is said the aircraft met an accident and Subhas was killed on 18 August 1945. But it could not satisfy his countrymen. The Government of free India set up a fact finding commission many times but it was of no use. The doubt is persisting. But Subhas is a hero in the hearts of millions of people. At that crucial moment, the shadow of this great man descended on the Indian stage like a colossus. Subhas Bose in absentia and his defeated Indian Army transformed the entire Indian situation. Despondency and frustration that had griped the ranks disappeared and the message of the lost leader and vanquished army opened the flood gates of an unprecedentedly united national movement for Independence of India. This post war mass upsurge was truly and completely national, in that it involved as never before, even such sectors of Indian population as had till then been immune to patriotic appeal, viz, the administrative services of all ranks, police and last but not least the armed forces. Had Subhas returned to India the history of his Subcontinent would have taken a different shape.

A new tradition was added to the history of India's freedom movement the military tradition of India's freedom fighters. The provisional government of Azad Hind (free India) gave to the Indian people the first experience of independence not statehood of two centuries of servile existence.

As a human being and a thinker, apart from being a political activist in the Indian national movement, Subhas Chandra Bose was seeking a new philosophy and a new ethical conception in the human affairs. A rare personality in contemporary history he was seeking a synthesis between the great spiritual heritage of India and modern technology with a view evolving a new social system in his country. His sense of mission did not admit any compromise or reservation. He sought to inspire his countrymen and followers by his own example of total dedication to the national cause. In this, he succeeded to a great measure and thus remains an example in leadership. His legacy in thought and deed for the present and coming generations remains. May India be worthy of that legacy and in the words of Subhas – Deliver to the world the message that has been her heritage through the past ages. While in Germany he married an Austrian women, Emile and had a daughter Nita, who has been visiting India from time to time.

Really, Subhas Chandra Bose was a great person who scarified his career and life for the motherland.

Plato

PLATO was a Greek Philosopher born in Athens in the year 428 BC. His father was Ariston who traced his descent from a king of Athens, Codus. His mother was Perictione whose family boasted of a relationship with the famous law maker of Athens and lyric poet Solon. Besides Plato himself, his father Ariston and his mother Perictione had three other children. They say, when Socrates was gone, Plato joined Cratylus the Heracleitean and Hermogenes who philosophized in the manner of Parmenides. At the age of 28, he went to Euclides in Megara. There is a legend that when Plato was an infant and was sleeping honey bees settled on his lips which is the augury of the sweetness of style in which he would discourse philosophy.

His father died in his childhood and his mother remarried her mother's brother. Although basically, he was named Aristocles after his grandfather, but his wrestling coach Ariston of Argos named him Platon, meaning 'broad' on account of robust figure. Later he became Plato who derived the name from breadth of his eloquence or else because he was very wide across the forehead.

Speusippus praised Plato's quickness of mind and modesty as a boy and the first facet of his youth infused with hard work and love of study.

Plato must have been instructed in grammar, music and gymnastics by most distinguished teachers of the time. It is told that he wrestled at the Isthmian games. He also attended the course of philosophy before meeting Socrates Plato makes clear that he was a devoted young follower of Socrates.

He never speaks in his voice in his dialogues. He may have travelled to Italy, Sicily, Egypt and Cyrene and returned to Athens at the age of forty and set-up his school on a plot of land in the Grave of Academus. Later, he was entangled with the politics of the city of Syracuse. During his first trip, the brother-in-law of the ruler became his disciple. But later on, this very disciple sold Plato as a slave. He almost faced death in Cyrene but an admirer purchased his freedom and sent him home.

Plato's Philosophy

Plato often discusses the father-son relationship and the question of whether a father's interest in his sons has much to do with how well his sons turn out. A boy in ancient Athens so socially located by his family identity and Plato often refers to his characters in terms of paternal and fraternal relationships. Socrates was not a family man and saw himself as the son of his mother who was apparently a midwife, a divine fatalist. Socrates mocks men who spent exorbitant fees on tutors and trainers for their sons and repeatedly, ventures the idea that good character is a gift from the gods. Crito reminds Socrates that orphans are at the mercy of chance but Socrates is unconcerned. In the Theaetetus, he is found recruiting as a disciple a young man whose inheritance is squandered. He twice compares the relationship of the older man and his boy lover to the father son relationship and in Phaeodo, Socrates disciples, towards whom he displays more concern than his biological sons, say they will feel 'fatherless' when he is gone.

Plato advocates a belief in immortality of the soul and several dialogues end with long speeches imagining the afterlife. More than one dialogue contrasts with knowledge and opinion, perception and reality nature and custom and body and soul.

Theory of Forms

The Theory of Forms typically refers to the belief expressed by Socrates in some Plato dialogues, that the material world as it seems to us is not the real world but only an image or copy of the real world. He sometimes seems to recognise two worlds, the apparent world which constantly changes and an unchanging and unseen world and of forms, which may be a cause of what is apparent.

Many have interpreted that Plato as stating that knowledge is justified true belief, an influential view that informed future developments in modern analytic. His epistemology. This is based on a reading of the *Theaetetus* where Plato argues that belief is to be distinguished from knowledge on account of justification. Many years later, Edmund Getter famously demonstrated the problem of the justified true belief account of knowledge. This interpretation however, imports modern analytic and empiricist categories on to Plato himself and is better read on its own terms than as Plato's views.

In the *Sophist*, *Statesman*, *Republic* and *Parmenides*, Plato himself associates knowledge with the apprehension of unchanging forms and their relationship to one another. More explicitly, Plato argues himself that knowledge is always proportionate to the realm from which it is gained. In other words, if one derives one's account of something experimentally, because the world of sense is in flex, the views therein, attained will be mere opinion and opinions are characterized by a lack of necessity and stability. On the other hand, if one drives one's account of something by way of the non-sensible forms, because these forms are unchanging so too is the account derived from them. It is only in this sense, that Plato uses the terms knowledge.

Plato's philosophical views had many social implications especially on the idea of an ideal State or Government.

There is some discrepancy between his early and later views. Some of the most famous doctrines are contained in *Republic* during his middle period as well as in laws and statesman. However, because he wrote dialogues it is assumed that Socrates is often speaking for Plato. This assumption may not be true in all the cases.

Plato, through the word of Socrates asserts that societies have a tripartite class structure corresponding to the appetite/spirit/reason structure of the individual soul. The appetite/spirit/reason stand for different parts of the body. The body parts symbolize the castes of society.

Productive, which represents the abdomen (workers) – labourers, carpenters, plumbers, masons, merchants, farmers etc. These correspond to the appetite part of soul. Protective, which represents chest – those who are adventurous, strong and brave in the armed forces. These correspond to the spirit part of the souls governing which represents the head those who are intelligent rational, self controlled, in love with rational, well suited to make decisions for the community. These correspond to the reason part of the soul and are very few.

According to this model the principles of Athenian democracy (as it was in his days), are rejected as only a few are fit to rule. Instead of rhetoric and persuasion, Plato says reason and wisdom should govern. As Plato puts,

> "Until philosophers rule as kings or those who are now called kings and leading men genuinely and adequately philosophise, that is until political power and philosophy entirely coincide, while the many natures who at present pursue either one exclusive are forcibly prevented from doing so critics will have no rest from evils … nor I think human race."

He describes these 'Philosopher kings' as those who love the sight of truth and support the idea with the analogy of a captain and his ship or a doctor and his medicine. According to him, sailing and health are not things that everyone is qualified to practise by natured large part of the republic then addresses how the educational system should be set-up to produce these Philosopher kings. However, it must be taken into account that the ideal city outlined in the republic is qualified Socrates as the luxurious city, examined to determined how it is that in justice and justice grow in a city. As per Socrates, the true and healthy city is, instead the one first outlined in book II of the *Republic*, containing, farmers, craftsmen, merchants and wage earners, but taking the guardian class of philosopher kings as well as delicacies such as perfumed oil's incense, pastries and prostitutes in addition to painting, gold, ivory, couches a multitude of occupations such as poets and hunters and war. In addition, the city is used as an image to illuminate the state of one's soul or the will reason and desires combined in the body.

He is attempting to make an image of a rightly ordered human and then later goes on to describe the different kinds of humans that can be observed from tyrants to lovers of money in various kind of cities. The ideal city is not promoted but only used to magnify the different kinds of individual humans and state of their soul. However the philosopher king image was used by many after Plato to justify their personal political beliefs. The philosophic soul according to him has reason, will, and desires united in various harmony. A philosopher has the moderate love of wisdom and courage to act according to wisdom. Wisdom is knowledge, the good and the right relations between all exits.

Wherein, it concerns states and rulers, Plato has made interesting arguments. For instance, he asks which is better – a bad democracy or a country reigned by a tyrant. He argues that it is better to be ruled by a bad tyrant than by a bad democracy. This is emphasised within *Republic* as he describes the event of mutiny on board a ship. He suggests the ship crew to be in line with the democratic rule of many and the captain although in habituated through ailments, the tyrants.

His description of this event is parallel to that of democracy within state and the inherent problems that arise.

According to him, a state made of different kinds of soul well, overall, decline from an aristocracy to a timocracy (rule by the honourable's) then to oligarchy (rule by the few) than to a democracy and to tyrant. Aristocracy is the form of government advocated in his *Republic*. This regime is ruled by philosopher king and thus, is grounded on wisdom and reason. The aristocratic state and the men whose nature corresponds to it, are the objects of Plato's analyses throughout his *Republic*, as opposed to other four types of states men, who are discussed later in his work. In book VIII Plato states in order to the other four imperfect societies with a description of the states structure and individual character, in democracy the ruling class is made up primarily of those with warrior like character. In his description Plato has Sparta in mind. Oligarchy is made of society in which wealth is the criterion of merit and wealthy are in control. In democracy the state bears resemblance ancient Athens with traits such as equality of opportunity and freedom for individual to do as he likes. Democracy then degenerates into tyranny from the conflict of rich and poor. It is characterized by an undisciplined society existing in chaos, where the tyrant rises as popular champion leading to the formation of his private army and growth of oppression.

Dialectic

The role of dialectic in Plato's thought is contested but there are two main interpretations, a type of reasoning and a method of intuition. His one dialectic is the process of eliciting the truth by means of questions aims at opening out what is already implicitly known or at exposing the contradictions and muddles of an opponent's position.

The Dialogues

Thirty-six dialogues and thirteen letters have traditionally been ascribed to Plato. But the modern scholars doubt the authenticity of at least some of these. His writings have been published in several fashions. This has led to several conventions regarding the naming and referencing of his texts.

The usual system for making unique references to sections of the text by him derives from a 16th century edition of Plato's works by Henricus Stephanus. An over view of his writing according to this system can be found in the Stephan's pagination article. One tradition regarding the arrangement of Plato's texts is according to tetralogics. This scheme is ascribed by Diogenes Lucretius to an ancient scholar and court astrologer to Tiberus named Thrasyllus. In the list below, works by him are marked (1) if there is no consensus among scholars as to whether Plato is the author and (2) if most scholars agree that Plato is not the author of the work unmarked works are assumed to have been written by Plato:

1. Euthyphro, Apology (of Socrates) Crito
2. Cratylus, Theactetus, Sophist Statesman
3. Parmenides, Philebus, Symposium
4. First Alcibiades (i) Second Alcibiades (2) Hipparches (2) Lovers (2)
5. The ages (2), Charmides, Laches, Lysis.
6. Euthydemus, Protagoras, Gorias, Memo
7. Hippias (1) Hippias (Lesser), Lon Menexenus
8. Clitopon (i) Republic, Timacus Critias
9. Minos (2), Laws, Epomomis (2) Epistles

The remaining works were transmitted under Plato's name, most of them already considered spurious in antiquity and so were not included in his tetralogical arrangement.

Composition of Dialogues

No one knows the exact order Plato's dialogues were written in, nor the extent to which some might have been later revised and written.

Increasingly, in the most recent Plato scholarship writers are sceptical of the notion that the order of the Plato's writings can be established with any precision, though his works are still often characterized as falling at least in three groups. The following represents one relatively common such division. It should, however, be kept in mind that many of the positions in ordering are still highly disputed and also that the very notion that his dialogues can or should be ordered is by no means universally accepted.

Among those who classify the dialogue, into period of composition, Socrates figures in all of the early dialogues and are considered the most faithful. The dialogues which are classified as early dialogues often conclude in aporia – the middle dialogues provide more clearly stated positive teachings of Plato – such as the Theory of forms. Some of the dialogues are very difficult to understand and challenging pieces of philosophy. These are the true testimony of Plato's mature thinking, although very difficult to discern the meanings.

Plato never presents himself as a participant in any of the dialogues with the exception of Apology. The unique thing is that there is no hint that he heard the dialogues first hand. Some of them have no narrator but have pure dramatic form. Some of them are narrated by Socrates himself wherein he speaks in first person. For example, one dialogue Protagoras begins in dramatic form but soon proceeds to Socrates narration of a conversation he had previously with the Sophist for whom the dialogue in name and this narration continued uninterrupted till the dialogues end. Similarly, two dialogues Phaedo and Symposum begin in dramatic form then proceed to virtually uninterrupted narration by followers of Socrates. Phaedo, an account of Socrates final conversation and himlock drinking is narrated by Phaedo to Echecrates in a foreign city not long after the execution of Socrates took place. Some of the dialogues are in such a form by which it seems that the narrator was an infant and not from his own memory.

Trial of Socrates

The trial of Socrates is the central theme and unifying event of great platonic dialogues. Because of this Plato's *Apology* is most read dialogues. In *Apology* Socrates tries to dismiss the rumours that he is a Sophist and defends himself against the charges of disbelief in the Gods and corruption of the youth. Socrates insists that long standing slander will be the real cause of demise, and says the legal charges surely false. Socrates famously denies being very wise and explains how his life as a philosopher was launched the Oracle at Delphi. He says that his quest to resolve the riddle of the oracle put him at odds with his fellow men and that this is the reason he has been mistaken for a menace to the city – State of Athens.

If Plato's important dialogues do not refer to Socrates execution explicitly, they allude to do it or use characters and themes that play a part in it. In one of the dialogues, one of the men who brings legal charges against Socrates, Anytus, warns him about the trouble he may get into if he does not stop criticizing important people. At this, Socrates says that his trial will be like a doctor prosecuted by a cook who ask the jury of children to choose between the bitter mediation of the doctor or the cook's tasty treat.

Platonic Scholarship

Although their popularity has fluctuated over the years, the works of Plato have never been without readers since the time they were written. Plato's thought is often compared with that of his most famous student, Aristotle, whose reputation during the western middle Ages so completely eclipsed that of Plato that the scholastic philosophers referred to Aristotle as philosopher. However, the study of Plato continued in the Byzantine Empire. His original writings were essentially lost to the western civilization until they were brought from Constantinople in the century of its fall. It is believed that Plethon passed a copy of the dialogues to Cosimo de Medic when in 1438 the council of Ferrara called to unify the Greek and Latin Churches.

These scholars not only translated the texts of the ancients but expanded them by writing extensive commentaries and interpretations on Plato's works.

Only in the Renaissance with general resurgence of interest in classical civilization, did knowledge of Plato's philosophy became wide spread again in the west. Many of the greatest early scientists and artists who broke with scholasticism and fostered the flowering of Renaissance, with support of Plato inspired Lorenzo de Medici saw Plato's philosophy as basis of progress in the arts and sciences. By the 19th century Plato's reputation was restored.

Death of Plato

A variety of sources have given accounts of Plato's death. One story based on mutilated manuscript suggests Plato died in his bed whilst a young Tracian girl played the flute to him, in the year 347 BC Another account is that he died in his sleep in Athens.

Plato was a Greek classical philosopher, mathematician and student of famous philosopher Socrates. He was the writer of philosophical dialogues and founder of Academy of Athens. The first institution of higher learning in the western world. Along with his mentor Socrates and his student Aristotle, he helped to lay the foundation of western philosophy and science every philosophical work of west must have a footnote of Plato. No doubt the scholars have extracted the Wealth of knowledge from his writings. Plato as a writer is evident in his Socrates dialogues 36 in all and thirteen letters. His writings have been published in several fashions. His dialogues have been used to teach the range of subjects including philosophy, logic, Ethics, rhetoric and mathematics. Plato is undoubtedly, the most important founding figure in western Philosophy. Therefore, he is a very great person of the world. His famous student was philosopher Aristotle of Athens and that too of Greek.

Aristotle

ARISTOTLE, whose name means 'the best purpose', was born in Stageira Chalcidice in 384 BC in Greece – 55 km east of modern day Thessaloniki. His father Nicomachus was the personal physician of king of Macedon. He was educated and trained as a member of the aristocracy. He went to Plato's academy at the age of 18. He remained there for 20 years. The traditional story of his departure reports that he was disappointed with the direction of the academy after it was taken over by Plato's nephew. He then travelled with Xenocrates to the court of his friend, Harnias of Atarneus in Asia Minor. While in Asia he travelled to Island of Hesbos and he did research in Botany and Zoology. He married Henmiar's adoptive daughter Pythias. She bore him a daughter, whom they named Pythias. He was invited by Philip–II to be the tutor of Alexander in 343 BC. He was appointed head of royal academy of Macedon. There he gave lesson to Alexander and two other future kings – Ptolemy and Cassandra he encouraged Alexander toward eastern conquests and his attitude towards Persia was unabashedly ethnocentric. In one famous example, he counsels Alexander to be a leader of Greeks and a despot to barbarians, to look after the former as friends and relatives and deal with the later as with beasts.

By 335 BC, he had returned to Athens establishing his own school known as Lyecum. He conducted courses there for twelve years. While in Athens, his wife Pythias died and he became involved who bore him son whom he named after his father, Nicomachus. It was during this period in Athens from 335-323 BC when he composed many of his works. He wrote many dialogues. The works that have survived are in treatise form and were not intended for widespread publication as they are lecture aids for students. His most important treatises include physics, metaphysics, ethics, politics and poetics. He not only studied most of the subjects but also significant contributions to most of them. He studied anatomy, astronomy, embryology, geography, geology and physics. He also studied foreign customs, literature and poetry. His combined works constitute a virtual encyclopaedia of Greek knowledge. He was perhaps the last person to know everything of his own time. Near the end of his life, he was known for not having no honour for the God. He fled to the town of his mother Calcis and said, "I will not allow the Athenians to sin twice against philosophy." It was with reference to the execution of Socrates. He died in Euboea in 322 BC. He left a will to be buried next to his wife.

Aristotle is credited with the earliest theory of formal logic and his conception of it was the dominant form of Western logic until 19th century advances in mathematical logic. Kant stated in the critique of pure reason that Aristotle's Theory of Logic completely accounted for the core of deductive inference.

History

He says, that on the subject of reasoning, he had nothing else on an earlier date to speak of. However, Plato reports that syntax was devised before him, by producers of Ceos, who was concerned by the correct use of words. Logic seems to have emerged from dialectics, the earlier philosophers made frequent use of concept like reduction and absurdum in their discussion but never truly understood the logical implications. Even Plato had difficulty with logic, although he had a reasonable conception of deductive he could never actually construct one and relied instead on his dialectical. Plato believed that deduction would simply follow from premises hence he focused on maintaining solid premises so that the conclusion would logically follow. Consequently Plato realized that a method for obtaining conclusions would be most beneficial. He never succeeded in devising such a method but his best attempt was published in his book *Sophist* where he used his division method.

Analytics and the Organon

What we today call Aristotelian logic he himself would have labelled 'analytics'. The term 'Logic' he reserved to mean dialectics. Most of his work is probably not in the original form since it was most likely edited by students and later lecturers. His logic works were compiled into six books in about early first century AD:

1. Categories
2. On interpretation
3. Prior Analytics
4. Posterior Analytics
5. Topics
6. On Sophistical Refutations

The order of the books is not certain, but this list was derived from analysis of Aristotle's writings. It goes from the basics analysis of simple terms in the categories, the analysis of proportions and their elementary relation in on Interpretation, to the study of more complex forms, namely, syllogisms and dialectics. The first three treaties form the core of logical theory *stricto sensu:* the grammar of the language of logic and the correct rule of reasoning there is one volume of Aristotle's concerning logic not found in the organon, namely the fourth book of *Metaphysics*.

Like his teacher Plato, Aristotle's philosophy aims at the universal. Aristotle, however found the universal in particular things which he called the essence of things. For him, therefore philosophic method implies the ascent from the study of particular phenomenon to the knowledge of essences. For him, form still refers to the unconditional basis of phenomena but is initiated in a particular substance. In a certain sense his method is both inductive and deductive.

His terminology 'Natural philosophy' is a branch of philosophy examining the phenomena of the natural world and includes fields that would be regarded today as physics, biology and other natural sciences. In modern times the scope of philosophy has become limited to more generic or abstract enquiries such as ethics and metaphysics in which logic plays major role. Today's philosophy tends to exclude empirical study of the natural world by means of the scientific method. In contrast, his philosophical endeavours encompassed virtually all facts of intellectual enquiry. In the larger sense of the word, he makes philosophy co-extensive – with reasoning, which he also would describe as science. Note, however that his use of the term science, carries a different meaning than that is covered by the term 'scientific method'. For him all science is either practical, poetical or the theoretical. By particle science, he means ethics and politics, by poetical science, he means the study of poetry and other arts, by theoretical science be means Physics, Mathematics and Metaphysics.

If logic is regarded as a study preliminary to philosophy, the division of Aristotelian philosophy would consist of – (1) Logic, (2) Theoretical Philosophy including Physics, Metaphysics and Mathematics, (3) Practical Philosophy, and (4) Poetical Philosophy.

In the period between his two stays in Athens, between his times at Academy and the Lyceum, Aristotle conducted most of the scientific thinking and research for which he is renowned today. In fact, most of his life was devoted to the study of the objects of natural science. His metaphysics contains observations on the nature of numbers. He did original research in the natural sciences e g botany, zoology, physics, astronomy, chemistry, metaphysics and several other sciences.

His writings are qualitative as opposed to quantitative, which provide an account of many scientific observations, a mixture of precocious accuracy and curious errors. He refuted Democritus claim that the milky way was made up of those stars which are shaded by the earth from sun's rays pointing out that given current astronomical demonstrations that size of the sun is greater than the size of the earth and distance of the stars from the earth many times greater than that of sun. Then the sun shines on all the stars and the earth screens none of them. His clarification of living things contains some elements which still existed in 19th century. What modern zoologist would call vertebrates, we called animals with bloods and animal without bloods. Animals with blood were divided into living beings human and mammals, and egg brings – birds and fish. Invertebrates are insects, crustacean and testacea.

He believed that intellectual purposes guided all natural process. Noting that "no animal has, at the same time, both tusks and horns," and "a single-hooved animal with two horns I have never seen." He suggested that nature giving no animal both horns and tusks was staving off vanity and giving creatures faculties only to such a degree as they are necessary. Nothing that ruminants had multiple stomachs and weak teeth – the first was to compensate the latter with nature trying to preserve a type of balance.

He also believed that creatures were arranged in a graded scale of perfection rising from plants on up to man. His system had 11 grades arranged according to the degree to which they are infected with potentiality expressed in their form of birth. The highest animals laid warm and wet creatures alive, the lowest bore their cold dry and in thick eggs.

He also held that the level of a creatures perfection was reflected in its form but not preordained by that form. He placed emphasis on the type of soul an organism possessed, asserting that plants possess a vegetative mobility and sensation and humans a vocative, a sensitive and a rational soul capable of thoughts and reflection. He placed the rational soul in the heart rather than the brain.

He holds that souls are three types: Sensitive Soul, Vegetative Soul and Rational Soul. Humans share the vegetative soul with all living things and sensitive soul with all animals but only humans in the world have the rational soul.

For him the soul was a simpler concept than it is today. By soul, he simply meant the form of a living being. Since all beings are composites of form and matter, the form of living being is that which endows them with what is specific to living beings, i e ability to initiate movement or in case of plants, growth.

He considered ethics to be a practical rather than theoretical studies, i.e. one aimed at becoming good doing good rather than knowing for its own sake. He taught that virtue has to do with proper function of thing. An eye is only a good eye in so much as it can see, because its proper function is sight. He reasoned that humans must have a function specific to humans and that this function must be an activity of the soul in accordance with reason. He identified such an optimum activity of the soul as the aim of all human deliberate action, generally happiness, well being. To have potential of ever being happy in this way necessarily requires a good character often translated as moral or ethical virtue.

He taught that to achieve a virtuous and potentially happy character requires a first stage of having the fortune to be habituated not deliberately but by teachers and experience, leading to later stage in which one consciously chooses to do the best things. When the best people come to live life this way their practical wisdom and intellect can develop with each other towards the possible human virtue the wisdom of an accomplished speculative thinker or in other words philosopher.

In addition to his works on ethics which addressed the individual, Aristotle addressed the city in his work. He considered the city to be a natural community. Moreover, he considered the city to be prior in importance to the family which in turn is prior to individual – the whole must be prior to a part. He also famously stated that man is by nature a political animal. He conceived politics as being like an organism rather than like a machine and as a collection of parts none of which can exist without the other. His conception of city is organic and he is considered first to conceive of the city in this manner.

The common modern understanding of a political community as a modern state is quite different to Aristotle's understandings. Although he was aware of the existence and potential of larger empires, the natural community was the city which functions as political 'community' or 'partnership'. The aim of the city is not just to avoid injustice or for economic stability, but rather to allow at least some citizens the possibility to live a good life and to perform beautiful acts. The political partnership must be regarded therefore as being for the sake of noble actions not for sake of living together. This is distinguished from modern approaches, beginning with social contact theory, according to which individuals leave the state of nature because of fear of violent death or its inconveniences.

He considered epic poetry, tragedy, comedy and music to be imitative, each varying in imitation by medium, object and manner. For example music imitates with media of rhythm and harmony, whereas dance imitates with rhythm alone, and poetry with language. The forms also differ in their object of imitation. Comedy for instance is a dramatic imitation of men worse than average, whereas tragedy imitates men slightly better than average. Lastly, the forms differ in their manner of imitation through narrative or character, through change or no change, and through drama or no drama, Aristotle believed that imitation is natural to mankind and constitutes one of the mankind's advantages over the animals.

While it is believed that his poetics comprised two books – one of comedy and one on tragedy – only the portion that focuses on tragedy has survived. Aristotle taught that tragedy is composed of six elements, plot structure character, style thought, spectacle and lyric. The character in tragedy are merely a means of driving the story and the plot, not the characters, is the chief focus of the tragedy. Tragedy is the imitation of action arousing pity and fear and is meant to effect the catharsis of those same actions. He concludes poetics with discussion on which, if either, is superior epic or tragic mimesis. He suggests that because tragedy possesses all the attributes of an epic possible possesses additional attributes such as spectacles and music, is more unified and achieves the aim of its memories in shorter scope it can be considered superior to epic.

He was a keen systematic collector of riddles, folklores and proverbs and his school had a special interact in riddles of the Delphic Oracle and studied the tables of Aesop.

Views on Women

Aristotle's analysis of procreation describes an active, ensuring masculine element bringing life to an inert passive female element. On this ground, feminists have accused Aristotle of misogamy and sexism. However, he gave equal weight to women's happiness as he did to men's and commented in his rhetoric that society can not be happy unless women are happy.

More than twenty three hundred years after his death Aristotle remains one of the most influential persons who has ever lived. He contributed to almost every field of human knowledge then in existence and he was the founder of many new fields. According to philosopher Bryan Magee,

> "It is doubtful whether any human being has ever known as much as he did. He was the founder of formal logic, pioneered the study of zoology and left every future scientist and philosopher in his debt through his contribution to scientific method. Despite these achievements the influence of his errors is considered by some to have held back science considerably. Bertrand Russell notes that almost every serious intellectual advance has had to begin with an attack on Aristotelian doctrine. Russell also refers to Aristotle's ethics as repulsive and calls his logic as definitely antiquated as

Ptolemaic astronomy. Russell notes that these errors make it difficult to do historical justice to Aristotle until one remembers how large of an advance he made upon all of his predecessors."

Aristotle influenced all the Greek philosophers Lyceums, Aristoxenus, Dicaearchus, Demetrius, Eudemos, Harpalus, Hephaestion, Meno, Mnason, Nicomachus, and Theophrastus. His influence on Alexander the great is seen in the latter's bringing with him on his expedition a host of scientists.

He had also learnt a great deal about Persian customs and traditions from his teacher. Greek Christian scribes played crucial role in the preservation of Aristotle by copying all the extant Greek language manuscripts of the corpus. The first Greek Christians to comment extensively on Aristotle were John Philoponus and David in sixth century and Stepen of Alexandria in the early seventh century. John Philoponus stands out for having attempted a fundamental critique of Aristotle's views on the eternity of the world movements and other elements of Aristotelian thought. After hiatus of several centuries formal commentary by Eustratius and Michael reappears in the late eleventh and early twelfth centuries, apparently by Anna Comnena.

Aristotle was one of the most revered western thinkers in early Islamic theology. Most of the still extant works of Aristotle as well as a number of the original Greek commentaries were translated into Arabic and studied by famous Muslim philosophers, scientists and scholars whatever was written on him, influenced the other scholars in great depth. Alkindus considered Aristotle as the outstanding and unique representative of philosophy and Averroes spoke of Aristotle as the exemplar for all future philosophers.

Medieval Muslim scholars regularly described Aristotle as the first teacher. The title teacher was first given to him by Muslim scholars and was later used by western philosophers who were influenced by the tradition of Islamic philosophy.

In accordance with Greek theorists, the Muslims considered Aristotle to be a dogmatic philosopher, the author of a closed system and believed that Aristotle shared with Plato essential tenets of thought. Some went as far as to credit Aristotle himself with neo-Platonic metaphysics ideas.

With the loss of the study of ancient Greek in the early medieval Latin west, Aristotle was practically unknown there from AD 600 to 1100 except through the Latin translation of the Organ made by Boetheus. In the twelfth and thirteenth centuries, the interest in Aristotle revived and Latin Christians had translations made, both from Arabic translations such as those by Gerayd of Cremona and from original Greek, such as those by James of Venice and William of Moerbeke. After Thomas Aquinas wrote his theology working from Morebike's translations, the demand of Aristotle's writings grew and Greek manuscripts returned to the west stimulating a revival of Aristotelianism in Europe that continued into the Renaissance.

Really, Aristotle was a great person because he contributed so much knowledge to the world as a whole which stood in good stead to humanity. He was not limited only to the philosophy, but he had thorough knowledge of every subject history, geology, physics, optics, metaphysics biology and medicine psychology, ethics, politics, rhetoric and poetry. It was not a simple study but he went very deep and deeper than to others of his times and even after him.

He influenced the common man, he influenced the kings, he influenced the scholars, he influenced the scientists and he influenced the historians. That influence was not superficial but of everlasting nature which is still casting its spell all over the whole world. Day in and day out he is being quoted at the time of debates of the highly educated persons and even in the highest Judiciary. It has been more than two centuries since he was on the earth but his works are still casting their spell all over the globe.

Aristotle had a daughter by his first wife and a son by his second wife who was given the name of his grandfather.

Rousseau

ROUSSEAU's full name is Jean-Jacques Rousseau. He was born on June 28, 1712 in Geneva. His father Isaac Rousseau was a watch maker and his mother was Suzane who died 9 days after his birth. His elder brother along with him were brought up by his father and a parental aunt, also named Suzane. When he was 5-6 years old, his father encouraged his love for reading.

Every night after supper, we read some part of a small collection of stories. My father's design was to improve my reading and he thought that this form of entertainment was calculated to give me fondness for it, but we soon found ourselves interested in adventure. They contained, that we alternately read the whole night together and could not bear to give over until at the conclusion of a volume. Sometime in the morning on hearing the swallows at our window, my father quite ashamed of this weakness would cry, "Come! come! let us go to bed, I am more a child than thou art."

But afterwards he abandoned the taste of the escapist stories in favour of antiquity of Plutarch's *Lives of Noble Grecians and Romans* which he would read to his father while he made watches.

At the age of 13 Rousseau was apprenticed first to a notary and then to a engraver who beat him. At age of 15 he ran away from Geneva.

He took shelter with a Roman Catholic priest in Savoy who introduced him to Francoise-Louise de Warens, a noble woman of 29 years. She sent the boy to Turen, the capital of Savoy to complete his conversion. At this he lost Genevan citizenship but later he regained it.

Finding himself on his own, since his father had more or less disowned him. He supported himself for a time as a servant, secretary and a tutor wondering in Italy and France. At a point he briefly attended seminary with the idea of becoming a priest. When he was 20, De Warens took him as her lover. He also took her as love of his life. She introduced him to the world of litters and ideas. During his 20s he applied himself in earnest study of philosophy, mathematics and music. At 25 he came to a small inheritance of his mother and used a portion of it to repay De Warens for her financial support of him. At 27 he took a job as a tutor in Lyon.

In 1742 he moved to Paris to present a new system of numbered musical notation, which he believed would make his fortune. But he was rejected by the academy, though he was praised for mastery of the subject. From 1743-1744 he had an ill-paid post as a secretary to Comte de Montaigu French ambassador to Venice where he fell for Italian music. But he left the job from experience a profound distrust of government bureaucracy.

He returned to Paris penniless and befriended and became the lover of Therese Levasseur who was the seamstress and sole support of her mother and numerous never to do well siblings. At first they did not live together. But later he brought them with him as his servants and himself assumed the burden of the whole the family. Before she moved with him she bore him a son. Along with the other children he was sent to a foundling hospital and became unknown, though Rousseau became famous as a theorist of education and child rearing.

At Paris he became the friend of French philosopher Diderot and contributed many articles on music to him, the famous of which was *Political Economy*, written in 1755.

His ideas were a result of an almost obsessive dialogue with writers of the past filtered in many cases through conversations with Diderot. His genius lay in his striking original way of putting things rather than in the originality, *per se*, of his thinking. In 1749 he paid daily visits to Diderot who was thrown into the fortress Vincennes due to his thinking which hinted at materialism, a belief in atoms and natural selection.

He participated in an essay competition to be published in *Mercure de France* on the theme of whether the development of the arts and sciences had been morally beneficial. He wrote, these are responsible for moral degeneration of mankind who were basically good by nature. He was awarded the first prize and he became famous.

He continued his interest in music. His opera performed for king Louis–XV in 1752. Impressed by this performance the king awarded him lifelong pension. But he declined the offer. This brought him notoriety – the man refused the pension from the king a great honour. He also turned down several after advantageous offers – some time causing him trouble.

In 1754 he returned to Geneva and regained the citizenship there. In 1755 he completed his famous work – *Discourse on the Origin and Basis of Inequality Among Men*. Then followed the composition of his three major works, in which he emphasized his fervent belief in a spiritual origin of man's soul and the universe. By dint of these works he enjoyed the patronage of two richest and powerful nobles of France.

His novel *Sentiments* of 800 pages was published in 1761 which brought him immense fame and success. In 1762 his work *Social Contract* was published which was very controversial. Even his friends took it otherwise. His work implied that the concept of Christian Republic was paradoxical since Christianity taught submission rather than participation in public affairs. In May his work *Emile* was published in which he defended faith in religion but somehow, it rejected original sin and divine revelation, both protestants and Catholics took offence. Moreover he advocated that, insofar as they lead people to virtue, all religions are equally worthy and that people should therefore conform to the religion in which they have been brought up. At this he and his books were banned in France and Geneva. His books were burnt and a warrant of arrest was issued but he managed to flee to Britain.

A sympathetic British philosopher David Hume professed no surprise when he learned that his books were banned in Geneva and elsewhere. He wrote that Rousseau has not had the precaution to throw the veil over his sentiments and as he scorns to dissemble his contempt for established opinions, he could not wonder that all the zealots were in arms against him. To be popular is very dangerous. Rousseau who thought that he was defending the religion was crushed. His friends helped him to publish his books again in Holland. These were distributed in France disguised as other works using false covers and title pages.

In Britain he took refuge with Hume who found a lodging for him at a friend's country estate in Staffordshire. He could not know English. Therefore he was isolated and he became emotionally unstable and his health declined. Once Hume wrote to a friend, "He is plainly mad, after having long been maddish. This was also published in France and was read with great interest."

He went back to France in 1767 under a fake name. He formally married Therese – his housekeeper. Though she was illiterate but she was a good cook and a companion for Rousseau because she shared his hobby.

In 1770 they were formally allowed to return to Paris but he was not allowed to publish any book. But after completing his book *The Confessions*, Rousseau began private readings in 1771. But the police stopped him. Thus *Confessions* published in 1782 four years after his death. All his subsequent works were to appear posthumously.

In the year 1772 he was invited to present recommendations for a new constitution of Polish-Lithuanian commonwealth, resulting in the considerations on the government of Poland which was to be his last major work. In 1776 he completed *Dialogues: Rousseau Judge of Jean-Jacques* and began work on the *Reveries of the Solitary Walker*. In order to support himself he returned to copying music, spending his leisure time in the study of Botany.

Final Years

Although he was a celebrity, his mental health did not permit him to enjoy his fame. His final years were largely spent in deliberate withdrawal. However he did not respond favourably to an approach from the composer Gluck whom he met in 1774. Gluck admired him as a pioneer of the expressive natural style in music. One of his writings was a critical yet enthusiastic analysis of Gluck opera Alceste. While taking a morning walk on the estate of the marquis Rene Louis de Giradin at Ermenonville (22 miles from Paris) he suffered haemorrhage and died, aged 66.

He was initially buried at Ermenonville on the Peupliers, which became a place of pilgrimage for his admirers. Sixteen years after his death his remains were moved to the Pantheon in Paris in 1794 where they are located directly across his contemporary Voltaire. His tomb in shape of rustic temple, on which in bas relief an arm reaches out bearing the torch of liberty, evokes Rousseau's deep love of nature and of classical antiquity. In 1834 the Genevan Government erected a statue in his honour on the tiny Ile Rousseau in Lake Geneva and he is proudly claimed as their most celebrated son. In 2002, the Espace Rousseau was established at 40 Grand-Rue, Geneva, his birth place.

Theory of Natural Human

The first man who, having fenced in a piece of land, said "This is mine," and found people naive enough to believe him, that man was the true founder of civil society. From how many crimes, wars, and murders, from how many horrors and misfortunes might not any one have saved mankind, by pulling up the stakes, or filling up the ditch, and crying to his fellows: Beware of listening to this impostor; you are undone if you once forget that the fruits of the earth belong to us all, and the earth itself to nobody. (This was said by Rousseau in his *Discourse on Inequality* in 1754.)

In common with other philosophers of the day, Rousseau looked to a hypothetical State of Nature as a normative guide.

Rousseau holds that 'uncorrupted morals' prevail in the 'state of nature' and he especially praised the admirable moderation of Caribbean's in expressing the sexual urge despite the fact that they live in the hot climate which always seems to inflame the passions.

He asserted that the stage of human development associated with what he called 'Savages' was the best and most optimal in human development between the less than optimal extreme of brute animals on the one hand and the extreme of decadent civilization on the others. Nothing is so gentle as the man in his primitive state when placed by nature at an equal distance from stupidity of brutes and the fatal enlightenment of civil man. Referring to the state of human development which he associates with savages, he writes: Hence, although man had become less forbearing, and although natural pity had already undergone. Some alternation in this period of the development of human faculties maintaining middle position between the indolence of our primitive state and petulant activity of our egocentrism, must have been the happiest and most durable epoch. More one reflects on this more one finds that this state was the least subject to upheavals and the best for man, and that the must have felt it only by virtue of some fatal chance happening, that for common good, ought never have happened. The examples of savages almost whom have been found in this state seems to confirm that the human race had been made to remain in it always, that this state is the veritable youth of the world and that all the subsequent progress has been in appearance so many steps towards the perfection of the individual and in fact towards the decay of the species.

Stage of Human Development

Rousseau believed that the savage stage was not the first stage of the human development but the third stage. He holds that this third stage of human societal development was an optimum between extreme of the state of brute animals and animal – like an 'ape man' on the one hand, and the extreme of a decadent civilized life on the other. This attributed to him the invention of the idea of the noble savage.

In fact, his natural man is virtually identical to a solitary chimpanzee or another ape and the natural goodness of humanity is thus the goodness of an animal which is neither good nor bad. He proposed that of except perhaps for brief moments of balance, at or near its inception, when a relative equality among man prevailed, human civilization has always been artificial creating inequality, envy and unnatural desires.

In his philosophy, society's negative influence on men centers on its transformation a positive self-love in to a pride. Positive self-love represents the instinctive human desire for self-preservation combined with the human power of reason. In contrast, pride is all artificial and encourages man to compare himself to others, thus creating unwarranted fear and allowing man to take pleasure in the pain and weakness of the others. In his discourse on Art of Sciences, Rousseau argues that the arts and sciences have not been beneficial to human kind, because they arose not from authentic human needs but rather as a result of pride and vanity.

Moreover, the opportunities they create for idleness and luxury have contributed to the corruption of man. He proposed that the progress of knowledge had made governments more powerful and thus had crushed the liberty and he concluded that material progress had actually undermined the possibility of true friendship by replacing it with jealousy, fear and suspicion.

In contract to the optimistic view of the other enlightened persons Rousseau, progress has been inimical to the well-being of humanity, that is, unless it has been counteracted by the cultivation of civic morality and duty.

Only in civil society can man be ennobled – through the use of reason:

> The passage from the state of nature to the civil state produces a very remarkable change in man, by substituting justice for instinct in his conduct, and giving his actions the morality they had formerly lacked. Then only, when the voice of duty takes the place of physical impulses and right of appetite, does man, who so far had considered only himself, find that he is forced to act on different principles, and to consult his reason before listening to his inclinations. Although, in this state, he deprives himself of some advantages which he got from nature, he gains in return others so great, his faculties are so stimulated and developed, his ideas so extended, his feelings so ennobled, and his whole soul so uplifted, that, did not the abuses of this new condition often degrade him below that which he left, he would be bound to bless continually the happy moment which took him from it for ever, and, instead of a stupid and unimaginative animal, made him an intelligent being and a man. (*Discourse on Inequality*)

Rousseau says that the society corrupts the men only in so far as the social contract has not de facto as we see in contemporary society. He traces man's social evolution from a primitive state of nature to modern society the earliest solitary humans possessed a basic drive for self-preservation and a natural disposition to compassion or pity. They differed from animals, however in their capacity for a free will and their potential perfectibility. As they began to live in groups and form clans, they also began to experience family love, which Rousseau saw as the source of greatest happiness known to humanity.

As long as the differences in wealth and status among families were minimal, the first coming together, in groups was accompanied by a floating golden age of human flourishing the development of agriculture, metallurgy, private property and division of labour and resulting dependency on one another, however led to economic inequality and conflict. As population pressure forced them to associate more and more closely, they underwent a psychological transformation as they began to see themselves through the eyes of others and came to value the good opinion of others as essential to their self-esteem. Rousseau posits that the original, deeply flawed Social Contract which led to the modern state, was made at the suggestion of the rich and powerful who tricked the general public into surrendering their liberty to them and instituted inequality as fundamental feature of human society.

At the end of *Discourse on Inequality*, he explains how the desire to have value in the eyes of others comes to undermine personal integrity and authenticity in a society marked by inter dependence and hierarchy by in the last chapter he asks "What is to be done?" He answers that now all men can do is to cultivate virtue in themselves and submit to their lawful rulers but it all seemed that new and more equitable Social contract was needed. He was also very critical of Atlantic slave trade.

Political Theory

His most important work is *The Social Contract* which outlines the basis for legitimate political order within a frame work of classical republicanism. It was published in 1762, it became one of the most influential works of political philosophy in the western tradition. It developed some of the ideas mentioned in an earlier work *Discourse on Political Economy*. The treatise begins with the dramatic opening lines,

> "Man is born free, and everywhere he is in chains. Those who think themselves the masters of others are indeed greater slaves than they."

He claimed that the state of nature was a primitive condition without law and morality which human beings left for the benefits and necessity cooperation. As society developed division of labour and private property required the human race to adopt the institution of law. In the degenerate phase of society, man is prone to be in competition with his fellow men while also be coming dependent of them. This double pressure threatens his freedom survival. According to Rousseau, by joining together into civil society through social contract and abandoning their claim of natural right, individuals can both preserve themselves and remain free. This is because submission to the authority of the general will of the people as a whole guarantees individuals against being subordinated to the will of others and also ensures that they obey themselves because they are collectively, the authors of law.

Although he argues that sovereignty should be in the hands of the people, he also makes a sharp distinction between the sovereign and the government. The government is composed of magistrates, charged with implementing and enforcing the general will. The sovereign is the rule of law, ideally decided on by direct democracy in the assembly. He was opposed to the idea that people should exercise sovereignty via a representative assembly. The kind of republican government of which Rousseau approved was that of the city state of which Geneva was the model or would have been if renewed on Rousseau's principles. France could not meet his criterion of the ideal state because it was too big. Much subsequent controversy about his work has hinged on disagreement concerning his claims that citizens constrained to obey the general will are there by rendered free.

The notion of general will is wholly central to his theory of political legitimacy – it is however an unfortunately observe and controversial nation. Some commentators see it as no more than the dictatorship of the proletariat or the tyranny of the urban poor as seen in the French Revolution but he was not meant as it is. Where Rousseau emphasizes that general will exist to protect individuals against the mass, not to require then to be sacrificed over it. He is of course sharply aware that men have selfish and sectional interests which lead them to try to oppress others. It is for this reason that loyally to the good of all alike must be a supreme commandment by everyone not only if a truly general will is to be needed but also if it is to be formulated successfully in the first place.

Education and Child Rearing

> "The noblest work in education is to make a reasoning man, and we expect to train a young child by making him reason! This is the beginning at the end; this is making an instrument of a result. If children understood how to reason they would not need to be educated."

Rousseau's philosophy of education is not concerned with particular techniques of imparting formation and concepts but rather with developing the pupils character and moral sense so that he may learn to practice self-mastery and remain virtuous even in the unnatural and imperfect society in which he will have to live. The hypothetical boy, Emile, is to be raised in the country side, which Rousseau believes is more natural and healthy environment than the city under the guardianship of a tutor who will guide him through various learning experiences arranged by the tutor.

Today, we call this disciplinary method of 'natural consequences' since, like modern psychologists. Rousseau felt that children learn right or wrong through experiencing the consequences of their acts rather than through physical punishment. The tutor will make sure that no harm results to Emile through his learning experiences.

He was the first to advocate developmentally appropriate education and his description of stages of child development mirrors his conception of the evolution of culture. He divides childhood into three stages. The first stage is up to 12, when children are guided by their emotions and impulses. During the second stage up to 16, reason starts to develop and finally during the third stage from 16 onwards, when child develops into adulthood. He recommends that the young adult learn a manual skill such as carpentry, which requires creativity and thought, will keep him out of trouble, will supply a fallback means of making a living in the event of change of fortune. The sixteen year old is also ready to have a companion of the opposite sex.

Although his ideas foreshadowed modern ones in many ways in one way they do not: Rousseau was a believer in the moral superiority of the patriarchal family on the antique Roman model. Sophia, the young woman, Emile is destined to marry, as a representative of ideal womanhood, is educated to be governed by her husband while Emile, as representative of an ideal man, is educated to be self-governing. This is not an accidental feature of his educational and political philosophy, it is essential to his account of the distinction between private, personal relations and the public world of political relations.

Religion

Having converted to Roman Catholicism early in life and returned to the austere Calvinism of his native Geneva as part of his period of moral reforms, Rousseau maintained a profession of that religious philosophy and of John Calvin as a modern lawgiver throughout his remaining life. His views on religion presented in his works of philosophy however may strike some as discordant with doctrines of both Catholicism and Calvinism.

At the time however, Rousseau's strong endorsement of religious tolerance, as expounded by the Savoyard vicar in *Emile*, was interpreted as advocating indifferentism, here and led to the condemnation of the book in both, Calvinist Geneva and Catholic Paris. His assertion in the social contract that true followers of Jesus would not make good citizens may have been another reason for his condemnation in Geneva.

In the 18th century, many deists viewed God merely as an abstract and an impersonal creator of the universe which they liked to gain machines. But his deism differed from the usual kind in its intense emotionality. He saw the presence of God in his creation, including mankind, which apart from the harmful influence of society, is good because God is good. His attribution of a spiritual value to a beauty of nature anticipates the attitude of 19th century Romanticism towards nature and religion.

He was upset that his deistic views were so forcefully condemned while those of the more atheistic philosophers were ignored. He defended himself against critics of his religious views in his letter to Christophe de Beaumont, in which he insists that freedom of discussion in religious matters is essentially more religious than the attempt to impose the belief by force.

Rousseau, who did not enjoy the love of his mother and who was almost abandoned by his father when he was just a boy, and who at the same time worked as a servant became very famous person of Europe in the field of music, education and philosophy. His books brought him laurels in his lifetime and he achieved greatness after his death. Many of his famous books were published after his death. The humanity as a whole gained from his philosophical findings and teachings when he was lunatic, he gave so many new ideas to the world. Therefore, he was a great person of the world. Although Rousseau married twice and he had a son from his second wife, the son could not survive.

Index